In the beginning

was the Word

and so shall it be again,

and the Word

is the Law,

and the Law

is Love.

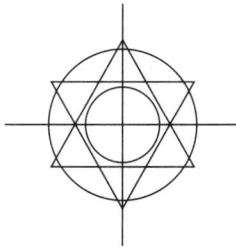

A Leaders of the Way book

From the same publisher:

The Way of Love
Joseph of Arimathea Tells the True
Story behind the Message of Christ
Compiled by Peter Wheeler
ISBN 90-75635-01-X. 256pp
(Also available in Dutch)

The Memories of Josephes
Soul Memories of a Cousin of Jesus
David Davidson
ISBN 0-9532007-0-1. 256pp

The Way of Crystals (Healing Handbook)
Joseph of Arimathea and the Prophet Elijah
Compiled by Zanne Findlay
ISBN 0-9532007-5-2. 160pp

The Children of Light (Monograph)
Father Abraham
Compiled by David Davidson
ISBN 0-9532007-2-8. 96pp
(Also available in Dutch)

The Way of Soul Part 1 (Monograph)
Joseph of Arimathea
Compiled by David Davidson
ISBN 0-9532007-4-4. 128pp

Discourses with Malachi (Monograph)
Opening to Spiritual Guidance
David Davidson
ISBN 9532007-6-0. 128pp

In preparation:

The Way of Diet and Health
The Way of the Changing World

More details at the end of this book. For an order form
please send a stamped, self-addressed envelope to:
The Leaders Partnership, Box 16457, London, SW14 5WH.

THE WAY
OF TRUTH

Conversations with a Master of Light

Compiled by Graham Timmins

Cover design: Anatole Beams at Digital Media.
Cover illustration: Graham Timmins.

Thanks to: ED for making all this possible.
Judith Timmins without whose love and tireless efforts
this book would not have been completed.
Zanne Findlay for her clarity and dedication.
David Davidson for his inspiration, guidance and support.
Peter Wheeler for inspiration and generosity of spirit.
Josef Schmied for his steady support.
Anthony Felt for his perception and insights.

Published by The Leaders Partnership,
a non-profit publishing venture.
PO Box 16457, London, SE14 5WH, UK.
www.arimathea.com
ISBN: 0-9532007-3-6

First edition 2001. Printed in the UK
by Bath Press, Bath, BA2 3BL.
Set in 11 on 14 point Galliard.

To my wife, Judith

The Way of Truth

Contents

The Arimathean Foundation

The Arimathean Foundation has been established to promote and distribute the spiritual teachings of Joseph of Arimathea, Father Abraham and the Prophet Elijah, who currently speak through a deep-trance channel.

Our first publication, *The Way of Love,* is a biography of Joseph of Arimathea told through a mosaic of discussions he had with individuals about the past lives they lived during the time of Christ. Through these verbatim accounts he reveals the story of his family, the events surrounding his life and those of his nephew Yeshua, who was to become the Christ.

The second book, *The Memories of Josephes,* is an intimate account of the life of the elder son of the Arimathean and his relationship with Yeshua. As children they were cousins and playmates; as adults Josephes and Yeshua were companions and confidants. The brilliant images and descriptions that make up this book are memories of a past life, recalled during meditation by the author.

In addition to these major works, two smaller imprints have been established, the Monographs and the Healing Handbook series. The Healing Handbooks are designed to give those involved in healing and caring for others simple, practical insights, direct from spirit. This will help them, their clients and loved ones achieve optimum health. The first title, *The Way of Crystals,* gives unique and authoritative advice on the use of crystals for healing. The Prophet Elijah and Joseph of Arimathea, two Spiritual Teachers never before published on this subject, bring their profound understanding from the Atlantean civilizations which has been tailored to the needs of today.

The Monograph series was established so that talks on specific and topical subjects from the three Spiritual Teachers, as well as inspired writings from the Arimathean group, could be placed before the public.

The first in the Monograph series was *The Children of Light.* This publication comprises the contents of five hour-long discussions with Father Abraham, the spiritual leader of these children. He has set out the needs, purpose and vision of a generation of very old souls who, with our help and encouragement, will restore balance, harmony and spiritual understanding to a world that is teetering on the edge of disaster.

In the second of the Monographs, *The Way of Soul*, this time based on six talks, Joseph of Arimathea presents a major thesis on soul: what it is, where it comes from, its relationship to God and to humanity, the vital importance of soul in this age and most importantly the pathway of soul, known since the beginning of time as 'The Way'.

In *Discourses with Malachi* a new Spiritual Teacher is introduced to our publications. Over a period of four years Malachi spoke to David Davidson during meditation and the most illuminating parts of the dialogue are gathered in this book.

As Malachi prepares his charge for the tasks and opportunities he will have to face in the future, we see the ancient relationship between master and pupil played out. David, living in the world, having to struggle with the immediate trials and tribulations of life, is counterpointed by the thoughtful measure of Malachi. What makes reading *Discourses with Malachi* rewarding is the universality of the polemic. In David we see the limitations and shortcomings of humanity; in Malachi, the patience, wisdom and depth of spirit.

The Way of Truth is an explanation of the simple spiritual truths underlying some of the most perplexing scientific and existential riddles facing humanity today. In a series of conversations with a channelled Master of Light, Graham Timmins gradually enters into an *experience* of truth, an experience which the reader can participate in too. This book demonstrates clearly how a deep, spiritual understanding of truth can be fostered using the principles of love and relationship. In so doing it points the way forward to a new paradigm of comprehension, one that does not rely on the hard evidence of science before it can be believed but that relies on an altogether different source: the human soul. Beyond time, naturally related to all things past and present, the soul is at one with both God and life, in touch with both individual and collective mind, and above all, in harmony with the love of the Creator that sent it forth.

Foreword

The purpose of this book is to bring light to bear on some of the enduring and perplexing scientific and existential puzzles that confront humanity today. In a series of discussions between a Spiritual Master – channelled by a deep-trance, direct-voice medium – and Graham Timmins, the compiler of this book, the interplay between spiritual perspectives and scientific discovery reveals a third principle operating in creation, a principle which must be experienced to be understood.

But why now? After all, what can a Spiritual Master possibly add to what science has already discovered? The answer is, a great deal. A Spiritual Master can add wisdom, foresight, understanding; a perspective that is derived from a far larger vision than we mortals, who live and die in the blink of an eye, can comprehend. He can offer a vision that is based on countless lifetimes of experience, augmented by a depth and breadth of knowledge that can only be acquired in the dimensions beyond the confines of the physical body.

Joseph of Arimathea, the Master whose words are recorded in this book, is speaking now in order to lay the ground for the Aquarian Age, the Golden Age, the age of the risen Christ. It is an age that is already beginning to show up the limitations of our present beliefs and that will continue to challenge our thinking and ingenuity in unimagined ways. Who better to bring the perspective of spiritual truth to these problems than the man who was uncle and guardian to the young Yeshua, the boy who grew up to become Jesus the Christ?

Truth is rather cold without its companion, love. Truth and love need to go hand in hand, because too much of one without the other to provide balance is intolerable. This book reveals a great deal of truth about the nature of creation, about the crucial place of humanity as an integral part of creation and the particular relationship of humanity to God. What is harder to see in the printed lines is the love with which the words were spoken, the source of which embraces all. This love was audible to Graham, in the inflection, the tone and pace of the Master's voice, the emphasis and feeling at certain points. Now, even though the words are printed in a book, the love is still there, in the pattern of speech and turn of phrase. As you read the lines, perhaps that love will become audible to you, too.

Spiritual Teachers do not use logical, linear language to comprehend the truths of which they are aware. As far as we can ascertain, those truths are held rather more in patterns of vibration and colour which have meaning and can be directly understood and experienced. For us to understand this truth it has to be translated, through the vocabulary and understanding of the channel, into words that can be written down and printed. There are many different ways of approaching and describing spiritual truth; poetry, art, science, at best they all capture an echo of that beautiful and elegant realm that is the mind of God. The skill of the questioner in compiling a book like this is not in the use of the pen, brush or test tube but in asking the right questions, putting alternatives so the speaker can choose an explanation and expand on the theme.

In order to do this, Graham had to learn a whole new vocabulary of concepts and ideas from the language of science and physics. As you read this book, you will see how the dialogue that ensued, at first a little formal, becomes more and more fluent. Gradually Graham and the Master move beyond the polarity of teacher and questioner, beyond the polarity of spirit and physical worlds to a more mutual *experience* of truth. They actually do the very thing that their dialogue is attempting to describe. By walking alongside Graham as you read this book you, too, can enter into and experience the truths that the Master, Joseph of Arimathea, wishes to convey – truths that, once understood, will change the way you see the world.

David Davidson, Spring 2001

Introduction

What is truth? It seems a reasonable question in the light of the title of this book and yet how elusive is the answer! Throughout the world there are centres of learning where research and questioning of a most fundamental nature takes place across the whole range of human endeavour. Vast libraries record, in meticulous detail, the ever-expanding knowledge of the most creative intellects throughout history and yet, as individuals, do we feel any more enlightened about the process of life in which we are involved? Does the mere accumulation of knowledge confer wisdom?

Nobody can deny the benefits of the scientific enlightenment and the technology that it has spawned, but the wisdom to use this power well and to share the benefits with all mankind has often been sadly lacking. Whilst many of us live lives relatively unchallenged by the basic need to survive, there are still those who cannot take their survival for granted. Even in the developed world there is an increasing sense of unease as the environment of our planet begins to show signs of instability.

At the other end of the spectrum from the scientist is the seeker after spiritual or mystical knowledge, where enlightenment is the goal. What is this truth, and how does it differ from that obtained by scientific method? Here, it is the individual that moves through a process of awakening using his intellectual, physical, intuitive and spiritual resources in order to gain a subjective experience of truth. In this case the experience and insight gained by the individual cannot be transferred to another. This is a highly personal search.

In this book the subjects are approached from an altogether different perspective by introducing the ideas and teachings of an Ascended Master in spirit. We gain an insight into the experience of life from a more subtle level of creation: how reality manifests from the unmanifest potential of creative energy. The nature of God, the Creation, the mind, the soul, and the purpose of life are outlined for the reader so that a clearer understanding of the process of life is gained. This book also covers some of the wider metaphysical aspects of life, including planetary beings, the concept of parallel universes and the experience of time and space.

Through a series of conversations some of the basic concepts are explored, creating a framework within which we can move towards an understanding of the purpose of our lives and see the broader picture. It is my hope that the views gained from this broader perspective will allow us all to open to intuitive insights and a deeper understanding. Together they may enable us to harmonize the logical, intellectual and scientific approach with a more subtle spiritual knowledge, vital to the flow and purpose of the whole process of life.

To do this I have attempted, as best I could, to ask questions directly of spirit in order to gain a clearer insight into the nature of reality and how that reality affects every one of us.

The aim of this book is not to vilify science but to balance this empirical truth with a more holistic truth. By uniting and harmonizing the scientific and the spiritual we become whole, able to engage in the play and display of creative energy all around us and to understand that life on Earth is a precious experience. Understanding this may help to encourage us all to seek a position of balance between these two poles, thus creating the necessary harmony in which the Earth and mankind can move forward into a brighter future for all.

The structure of the book
The book first introduces our teacher from spirit and then moves into a set of conversations that ebb and flow across a wide range of topics, weaving a tapestry of knowledge and teaching in a very gentle way. There are many points of return as I struggled with the concepts and attempted to gain understanding, initially adopting a scientific approach which soon evolved into a more easy acceptance, thus providing a firmer basis for deeper truths to be revealed.

Throughout the conversations I have interspersed notes, (in bold text), revealing the insights I gained from the teachings and explaining the reasoning behind my questions. At the back of the book is an appendix containing a framework of teachings upon which the conversations are based. While not strictly necessary to the flow of the book, these extracts from earlier lectures define and explain, in a much fuller way, many of the concepts discussed in the conversations. Readers unfamiliar with such concepts may find it helpful to read this appendix before reading the main part of the book.

There is a practical application to this kind of knowledge, in that it encourages us to appreciate the power of the mind, how the way we think creates the world we live in. Using the Earth-healing meditation and visualizations detailed in Appendix II, you can benefit our environment and help restore balance to the planet by accessing the potential of the mind and by joining your energy with the many groups and individuals already engaged in this work.

Graham Timmins, Spring 2001

Introducing the Master

In order to achieve a much wider perspective, it is necessary to step outside our normal experience of life. In this book this perspective is provided by a group of Teachers in spirit, who reside on the causal plane. The causal plane is the level of being attained by those of great wisdom and knowledge who have completed their cycle of earthly incarnations and have gained mastery over the process of life on Earth. Having no need of a physical body, these souls have moved beyond the gross physical level to a more refined and enlightened sphere of life where their fulfilment comes from teaching and inspiring.

The group of Teachers whose knowledge is represented in this book all form part of one total soul, or Higher Self. Since this is an important tenet of the teachings and will be mentioned on several occasions, a brief extract from earlier teachings is included here to explain this concept:

The Higher Self

For those of you who are not totally aware of the meaning of the words 'the Higher Self', we wish to explain. All of you are aware of soul. You know that there is within you a soul which enables your spirituality to mature. It enters into you at birth and does not return permanently to the spirit world until the time of death of the physical body.

But where does it return to? The Higher Self is your total soul. In each life that you live upon the Earth, a different aspect of soul enters that fleshly body, an aspect which has not lived and learned before. At the end of the life, when it returns to the Higher Self, all the knowledge that has been gained is assimilated into that Higher Self. It is permeated with the understanding, the reality of that life. This process continues throughout eternity.

Already there have been two million years where the soul has returned in this manner, so you can imagine how many aspects there are within that total soul, the Higher Self – as many as cells within your body. But not all experience a spiritual life. There are some lives in which purely the physical and material are understood, and not all lives represent the truth and beauty which comes with spirituality. This is obvious within your world, when you see some of the wicked deeds which are done by those that are not pure in heart. But that soul must still learn. The soul cannot learn only through imbibing the truth. It learns through suffering – both its own and others'. It learns slowly and gradually to understand the truth of existence.

The causal plane
There comes the time when the soul no longer desires to go to the Earth world. It feels its lessons are learned and that it will now achieve more by travelling to the higher spheres.

The next stage is the causal plane. It [the soul] must be prepared to lose the etheric self, no longer to be aware of earthly contacts. It is a time of decision, for there is only going forward and no returning. They enter the portals where the light is so strong that only those who are able to achieve great heights of learning can pass beyond it and be absorbed into the light. Those who are not ready go back, but those who deserve the causal plane, those who can be the Masters and the Teachers, will go forward and will be absorbed into the light.

The causal plane is the plane of reality. It is the plane of all truth, all knowledge, all understanding, the culmination of the visual, of all the incarnations – the composite whole, where the soul understands itself and its part in life.

Our own guide is Joseph of Arimathea who, 2000 years ago, was the uncle and mentor of Christ. He had foreknowledge of his nephew's special quality because an angel visited him shortly before the birth and he was responsible for much of Jesus' upbringing and education. The story of Joseph and his family is contained in the sister publications, *The Way of Love* and *The Memories of Josephes*.

Joseph of Arimathea now acts as spokesman for a group of Teachers on the causal plane. In the early years of his teaching, he gave no name, saying only that he spoke on behalf of a much wider group, and it became the custom to address him simply as Master, as a sign of respect towards a teacher. In one of the earliest trances he briefly introduced himself to a new audience thus:

Master: First we will explain who we are. I am known as 'the Master' and I am the spokesman for a group of spirit people, who have lived many times in the Earth world and have followed the progression of their soul until it is no longer necessary to return to the Earth's surface. Lessons once learnt go to help the soul in its fulfilment. But until the soul is ready to join the spirit of all life, there must be a period of time in the spirit realms where it can learn even more, and absorb even greater knowledge, knowledge which the physical being in the Earth plane is unable to assimilate.

The group which we are have been in spirit now for many thousands of years, but we are still able to contact the Earth world and to speak through such as our channel, presenting to people who wish to know, the facts as we see them. We do not set ourselves out to be above all others in this field but we do feel that, through the thousands of years of coming and going in different incarnations, we are able to speak quite knowledgeably on many facets of life.

So it is in conversations with the Master that this book will present the nature of reality as it is viewed from the causal plane. Here he explains how those on the causal plane perceive our level of existence.

Questioner: I was wondering about the perception of the spirit world. You can see down to the smallest particles, atoms and within atoms – is there a limit to your resolution?

M: In theory, as we see everything as a vibration, we would answer yes. We do see these minute fragments. We would see atoms in that manner. What is infinitely more difficult for us is to be aware of objects in the way that you are. If you have in your possession a cupboard that is made of wood then we see the vibration from the wood reflected in it. So we see the outline and volume of the object; we see how much wood there is in it. We see those parts of the object that are not wood. If they are natural, then our perception of the energy which is within this other part would be different to that which is the wood. Anything that is made of plastic would be a void.

Those who are able to come to the Earth more often to be aware, as we are, for example, of that which is within the place where you are sitting, are able to distinguish what everything is composed of as we are able to see the vision through the channel's eyes. We can translate from the pure energy field into that which she perceives, not clearly, but we are able to determine the outline, to be aware in a more positive manner of what is taking place. With yourself we see each organ as it vibrates etherically, the crystals which are within the room, in fact any crystals which may be presented to us for our blessing. Each crystal vibrates differently from the others according to the gemmology from which it stems. If we are given an amethyst then that vibrates differently from clear quartz. In general, if we are speaking through our channel and we desire more understanding of her situation, where she is, if she is in danger for any reason, it is a more difficult perception for us in unfamiliar surroundings than in a known environment.

The old analogy, my son, of describing a mountain to a blind man comes in here, does it not? If you were able to perceive each natural object within this space, with its accompanying natural vibration, and to be aware of a total void where manufactured articles are concerned that have no natural energies within them, you would understand more deeply what we are sharing with you.

The descriptions of concepts can sometimes be rather tenuous as the Master can only use the vocabulary of the channel through whom he speaks. In this case the channel is not a scientist, nor an academic; nevertheless it is surprising what deep concepts may be described in simple terms. I see this as an advantage as, I hope, it helps make this book accessible to all, regardless of education or background. Here the Master explains how he uses the vocabulary of his channel to describe scientific concepts:

Q: *Can I use specific scientific terms and are you able to use and understand specific terms?*

M: That we have not been able to do. It is rather a complex situation. It does involve being able to understand that which our channel herself can evaluate, that which she has learned at different times within her life, however fragmentary it could possibly be. There are certain limitations to language and to descriptions which cause, of course, hesitancy when we are endeavouring to read her vocabulary in order to speak as we ourselves wish to. If we are unable to ascertain the correct word then we have to describe it in a different way.

Q: But you would understand what I am saying?

M: That is so; we would be able to answer yes or no if you place things in a certain descriptive way. We always find it very limiting when we wish to speak in a more scientific way but in general, with those that come and ask our guidance and in the subjects that we choose for group discussion, we find that we have no problem.

In an extract taken from the beginning of our discussions, the Master indicates the extent of the soul group involved in bringing forward the information for this book:

M: As we approached we were very aware of the atmosphere of concentration, and we might even add devotion, that met us as we linked with both your auras [myself and the channel] and began to understand the nature of what is required from us. On this occasion it is so very different from other forms of request for information and teaching. There are many involved within the spirit world in producing information of this kind for the book that the Arimathean group will be producing for the world. It is not just myself, Joseph, who is involved in this. In fact, the awareness of how many there are within the group that offer teaching and understanding of not only spiritual matters but those things which are very important within the material world might surprise many.

Chapter 2

Conversation One

*Energy and God. Mystical experience. The power of the
mind. The mind defined. Meditation. Levels of existence.
Consciousness. Consciousness and quantum theory.*

Energy and God

The Master teaches that God is a composite of a number of
aspects, one of which is an energy and that idea intrigued
me. Before my association with this teaching, I had not
thought of the nature of God as something scientific but
rather more spiritual and somehow beyond logic and the
empirical methods of science, more belonging to the
domain of experience, inspiration, faith and intuition. So I
was anxious to understand what the nature of this field was
and to see whether the definition might have a parallel in
sub-atomic physics.

*Please note: in these conversations, when talking about Jesus, the
Master always uses the name 'Yeshua', which was the affectionate
family name for his nephew.*

Master: Welcome, my son. Shalom.

Graham: *Welcome, Master. Shalom.*

M: We have long awaited this time with you, to be able to truly
start the discussion and awaken the teachings that are deep
within you, waiting, as it were, to be released. So much is
buried within your own subconscious. Although we expect that
the knowledge within the universe will be spoken by ourselves
over a period of time, this could not be achieved without the
supporting knowledge which is within those with whom we
speak – in this case, yourself. So now, my son, we are waiting
for your comments and for your first question.

G: *Thank you, Master. So, to begin, I have been reading some of
the teachings that you have delivered over the years and more
specifically I have been focusing on the subject of energy. I have
come across a chain of events in one of the teachings which goes
rather like this: God is energy, which becomes light, which in turn*

becomes force. So it would seem to me that you have the unmanifest becoming manifest in a very subtle form of energy, becoming more manifest in the vibrational form of light and then becoming a kinetic energy in the way of force or matter. Now, we have this expression 'God is love'. I can see how this continuum of energy could be called love, but is that love a different quality from what we as human beings know to be love and experience as love? I wonder if you can enlighten me as to what the nature of God is and whether love is, in fact, some scientific quality.

M: It is again, of course, a matter of words. The church teaches of the love of God mainly through using words attributed to Yeshua when He was upon the Earth and when He was endeavouring to release man from the fears that man had had for so many generations, of a vengeful God. A God who would bring down wrath, who would destroy. A God who would bring pestilence upon those that disobeyed.

Yeshua was a manifestation of the true love within God and He came in the form that He did, as a human being, to portray compassion, enlightenment and all the qualities that man himself could relate to. When He spoke of God the Father, it was in the language of those who would not have understood it had He referred to God as an energy field which supported the universe, which allowed each planet within the universe to remain in connection with each other and with, of course, the most important planet of all – the Earth. He had to choose His words most carefully, so that man could accept Him, firstly as part of God – God manifest in kinetic energy which holds human beings to the Earth. Also for man to accept that there is not the revenge element, which the more ancient Jewish tribes, and the people even before that time, accepted as their conception of God.

So the word love is a little out of place. Too often it is that which is used by mankind to express desire, and God is not an expression of desire. You can say that desire is within the nature of God. Within that nature there are all things which surround man's awareness – awareness of energy, of the movement of time, of his conception of space – and the rather scrappy teachings which have come down on a religious basis over so many thousands of years. We would relate the nature of God to that which is the total conception of life. We speak within our teachings of God being manifest in the wind, in the rain, and plant life, as well as animal life, and humankind. We speak of God being present even in the residue which becomes dust, even the mites that are of the lowest form of insect life that is within the world. But He is also within that which has brought about all planetary existence. He is within radiation and He is indeed within atomic structures that have more recently become part of science and scientific awareness. It is that atom which relates to all that lives, all that expresses, all that can respond in one way, whether to hearing, to touch, to taste or even within thought. But it is a moving energy; there is nothing that relates to the God aspect that is still.

Man's awareness when he speaks of the still small voice of God is his awareness of a quality, something that exists beyond his own personality and that he finds it so difficult to be aware of and then to describe. Even his thought is limited to what he has experienced within his life. That which he has never experienced, he would be unable to relate to. It is like a blind man deprived of sight from the moment of birth. Describing what is seen all around him means nothing unless he is able to touch it and work out for himself what he feels the object may be. With larger objects, which he is unable to encompass with his limited senses, he would not be able to comprehend their totality. It may sound trite but that God energy, which gives life, also allows the thought process to be so limited.

So you have a force that can be greater than any comprehension that comes through the power of thought, and you can also have that which is so infinitesimal that thought cannot relate to it, cannot pick it up. If you put both these aspects of greatness together then you have the total volume that represents the God simplicity and the God greatness and profundity. Put into a sentence, it means there is nothing universally outside of God. Whatever name you care to give to this energy, it still comes down to that particular point.

Before God existed

This raises the point of what existed before the universe was created. If this God energy existed before that breath took place and life was formed, where did it exist? In what form did it exist? And why was there not some manifestation of life in the universe before the scientific proof that has already been found. But has it? Do not the scientists always keep coming back to that initial vibration? Do they not keep finding more and more evidence of civilized man many hundreds and thousands of years before they first thought it was possible? Have they not, more recently, discovered what it was that killed the dinosaurs? And will they not go back even further and really discover that quality that created the Earth?

Eventually they might, but science limits. It does not allow that expansion of awareness that is necessary to understand the concept of forever and ever without end. The universe qualifies for this extremely limited expression of words; and yet it raises within the conscious mind this feeling of limitless power, limitless life which man cannot really accept because man is finite and therefore he cannot see that infinite that is presented to him. Even the soul aspect, when it is within the personality, cannot express total knowledge. Outside of it, when it is reaching throughout the universe in all its great beauty and awareness, then it accepts, because it is at one with that infinite and total expansive being.

Light always existed. There was never a time when it did not. Let man try and work his equations, he cannot prove this. Man manifests the quality of the light. He knows what makes up light itself. He knows what builds into darkness, but he cannot find its source. If he decides that this elusive God is what has provided this light, provided this movement upon the waters of life, he still cannot put either his experiments, nor yet his thoughts into going back into a space that has no end. When eventually the world ceases to be, the universe will still be present; the world will simply be dead flotsam within it. Life as it is known upon the Earth will continue somewhere else and that seed which is within it will always exist within the infinite being of God. Do our words make any sort of sense, my son?

Mystical experience

These comments brought to mind the experiences that can occasionally occur in practices such as Hatha yoga and meditation: a feeling of expansion, losing the boundaries and experiencing the joy of just 'being'. Likewise in quantum physics, there is a probability that a physical particle may be manifest anywhere in time and space.

G: *I can grasp the concept of the infinite being experienced rather than intellectualized. Our intellect is based upon words, and words are based upon our experiences. It appears to me that the infinite is something that maybe is closer to an experiential knowledge rather than an intellectual one.*

In science, man attempts to reduce things to their simplest level. You have things like the atom, proton, neutron, and electron, and there is an attempt to see what each particle is made of and how they are created, but rarely, why.

My understanding is that there is vibrational energy everywhere. But, in fact, the vibrational energies, which make up a particular particle in space and time, only manifest at one particular point. This is because the infinite energies destructively interfere at all other points except the point where the particle is manifest. Hence you get a physical presence at the particular point in space and time. In fact, it is everywhere because it is composed of these infinite waves.

From my own experience of it, albeit a very limited one, when one has an expansion of consciousness one can feel to be almost everywhere. I am not sure whether what I have experienced is what you have just described as the infinite presence of God.

Man and Earth

M: We feel that it is as near to that concept as man is able to go. There are certain elements within man, within his body, which of course relate totally to the Earth itself and to what comprises the Earth. That which is within man is of exactly the same quality, so man can only relate to his Earth. He cannot relate to any other planet, so life for him upon another planet simply could not exist. Man would have to create on that planet the exact conditions that he has upon the Earth to be able to stay there for any particular time at all. The further he goes into space, the more difficult it would be for his body to contain the energies that are within it. This is because the energies surrounding other planetary life are different. In very deep space, which has not yet been penetrated by man's probes, circumstances would not allow, in any way, for man to travel there without his body exploding.

It is in these matters that science falls apart. They are always trying to visualize what man himself can do to prove something: to go to a planet, to live there, or to be for a while upon its surface in order to probe how it is different from that which is on the Earth – or to be more accurate, how similar its components are to that of the Earth – without realizing that man's body could not stand the energy field that surrounds those particular planets. There is no protective clothing that could do this, the explosion would take place within that clothing and therefore there would only be particles left if the person were projected back to the Earth.

The power of the mind

Anyone who studies the nature of the mind is eventually introduced to the concept of the power of the mind. This is particularly true of the great spiritual teachers, both past and present. I have never been quite sure just what mind is or indeed what power actually resides there. I can see that the gift of free will is an absolute one in that we all have the power to create our own reality and also we have total responsibility for ourselves and our actions.

The Master goes well beyond this concept to the idea that by using our minds we can effect a vibrational change which can, in a very real sense, have profound effects. This is reminiscent of the mystical powers encapsulated in teachings such as the Yoga Sutras of Patanjali and other esoteric teachings where these apparently unearthly powers have been defined. It goes some way to explaining Yeshua's ability to walk on water, for example, or his ability to appear quite suddenly amongst His disciples.

Vibrational rates and the mind of man

There is one point here which may be helpful and that is that by raising man's vibrational rate, he could disappear before the eyes of those that are watching him, and he could then through his own thought vibrations appear somewhere else. Of course, before this can take place, he would have to be aware of his power of thought, and put away this limitation that he is born with, that he can only walk upon the surface of the Earth, and must perform certain rituals in order to remain alive. It would be such a shock to his nervous system to realize that, however briefly, he simply did not exist, that all the molecules and particles that make up his being have been fragmented. His mind would have to hold them all together so that when he reappeared elsewhere he would be in the same format. If his mind did not do this, on reappearing he would be a different object; he might not even be human at all.

Although science fiction is full of probabilities, none of these things could possibly begin to take place until science discovers the ability to change vibrational rates and apply them to thoughts within the mind of man.

The mind defined

In any discussion of the potential of the mind we, as rational, logical beings, need a definition of mind as our understanding in this area, even among scientists, is very sketchy. Here the Master defines the terminology and distinguishes between the physical brain, which is of the body, and the mind, which is a transcendent aspect connecting us with the soul and the universal mind.

It should also be noted that he defines spirit as the life force which animates the physical body and which enters the body at birth and returns to source at the point of death. This energy is universal and I see it rather as the charge in a battery which is used to power our machines.

Mind and brain

Mind cannot be seen within the body. Brain can, mind cannot, because mind is associated absolutely with the infinite God. The mind is a link and therefore it can expand endlessly, ceaselessly; it can relay back to the brain all the awareness of what the spiritual planes have within them.

All life still exists within these planes of light. All the past tribes of people, and past animals like the dinosaurs, still exist. All that occurred when they were extinguished from the Earth was the ability then for them to be transformed into another existence. During the very first civilization, man was able to transport himself from the spiritual spheres to the Earth at will, because the mind was less limited. It had been created as part of the God force and man was far more advanced than he is at this time. But of course he destroyed himself through limitation as the ages passed. He has, to a certain point, become less agile, less able to reason and to project knowledge. However, having reached the point of the spiral where he has become totally incapable, he is now beginning to ascend it once more. During this present age, and the age to follow, he will then reach that point of knowledge where he was indeed created and will have memory of the creation, as well as memory that he does have within himself, of physical birth.

Returning to the original statement which you placed before us, we do feel that you are very close to truth. As we continue to discuss with you and endeavour to project in words what those within the spiritual spheres know to be true, then perhaps man will begin his journey up the spiral with increasing ability for this infinite knowledge to be retained. After all it can be done. The atom is split and this is infinite so why should not mankind's ability to draw in knowledge from the infinite itself be made manifest?

Meditation
I was interested to hear the Master introduce the concept of a journey, implying that there was indeed room for expansion and progress. In the world of today we have the impression that we have achieved an apparent mastery over the material world and that all that remains to be done is just fine-tuning. However, the recent upheavals in many parts of the Earth indicate that our confidence in this matter is misplaced. The idea that we are, in fact, more primitive than former cultures is rather surprising and yet somehow not. After all, we live in many types of social and political groupings, none of which are ideal, and many people fall victim to exploitation, whether they are aware of it or not. The economic interests of the status quo often run counter to the health of humankind, the ecosystem and even the well-being of the planet. So I was particularly keen to know how this expansion could be achieved.

Fear and meditation
G: *How would mankind embark upon such a journey?*

M: We are always endeavouring to instil into those who come and speak with us the importance of meditation. Very few people realize that the only way to leave behind the matter that encases man is through linking solely with the mind. This is done by allowing oneself to move out of what the brain encompasses, beyond the words which are within his brain, beyond the limitations of sight which he has experienced. He must cease to try and interpret what he sees when in deep meditation, just to accept and not try to put a limit upon it by saying, 'This is evil, this is darkness, these are creatures that can destroy me. This is something that can prevent me from returning to myself, and living my life.' But just to accept that what comes with really deep meditation is the first step into the infinite.

There is one quality that we have not yet mentioned, and that is fear. Fear is what limits man in his experience and in his knowledge. The soul does not have fear; the God force does not know the meaning of fear because fear only exists in man's brain, not even in his mind. It is within his brain, his reality, it is what he sees, and feels, what he tastes. This brings about fear. The genetic being which is his body, experiences and projects fear through the different bodily fluids [hormones] and the contents of his organs that promote the fear response within the brain. When man says he is mindful of fear, it is a misnomer. It is when the unknown is presented to him that the body reacts, the organs react, and in that way his response is to withdraw and not go forward.

People could go much deeper into the world of trance, into the ability to elevate themselves in meditation if they could get through the fear barrier. But this, of course, means moving out of the barrier of matter and it cannot be done in the physical body. It is an endless circle, my son. It is that which exists, but that also which only exists within the outer perimeter of the universe. It cannot be penetrated by man. That is where the creation exists, where thought emerges, where the essence called God is in existence. We have spoken elsewhere of the energy patterns of the colour streams, and how they apply from that creative principal through to man. We think that will be a little clearer for you. [See page 151 in Appendix I.]

Levels of existence

The possibility opening up before me was that there may be levels of existence and experience of which many of us have no direct knowledge. I was anxious to discover where on this scale our reality lay, as it would appear that the other levels are far more powerful, harmonious and subtle than that of the physical universe which forms our own reality.

The link between man and Earth

G: Are we on the Earth inhabiting the densest form of existence? I seem to remember in one of your teachings on the Aum, that initially there was a sound vibration – in the beginning was the Word – which then manifested into the various levels of existence, and that the densest of these is mankind. Is that actually true, or is mankind a less dense form of creation than the Earth?

M: It is the same. That which makes up the Earth itself, all the same materials are in mankind and most of it is crystal based. Then you have the water base. After that you have a whole series of molecules which present themselves in different patterns, such as the bones and the flesh, the skin. They are all different organs but they are all replicated within the Earth itself – not necessarily in the same form as man but they are all there. [See *The Way of Soul* for a fuller explanation.]

Aum, the sound of the universe

Now, going back to the Aum, it emanated from the God force, it *is* the God force. This sound, this projection of energy making the sound as it approaches the Earth, would not actually be heard or experienced in any way in this outer level of existence of which we speak. In that existence, it purely is. This has to be accepted as a point of reference, a point of beginning: that everything to do with the Creative Principle *is*. You have to start from that, you cannot go earlier than that because there is nothing earlier except an infinite progression back and back and back until you find yourself coming around again to meet yourself. So the total circle of the God force is constantly spinning, constantly reverberating within everything that is in existence. As it does this, that which *is*, becomes consciousness. And within that consciousness, as it approaches where mankind's thoughts and mind can penetrate, it resonates as sound.

If you go to a plateau on a high mountain, where absolutely nothing else can be replicated within man's ears, first within his head he would hear the rhythm of this vibration. Then as he tunes in very finely to the vibration, it becomes manifest as sound until it is almost deafening in its rise and fall. It is only detectable when nothing else interferes. You can have awareness of it when you are meditating because it is that very important vibration within the self that comes with utter silence. There can be a great amount of noise outside but within the space where the meditator is sitting there is that infinite silence which is the soul. He has tuned into the soul, and therefore he has tuned into the Aum.

Soul exists beyond this barrier because the soul is part of the infinite Creator. This is why man can relate to this and why the planetary existence relates in a different way, and has a different vibration, and different awareness – without brain, because there is no substance and there is no personality. Those that exist on a planetary level can only be particles of light; they cannot be anything different. As a particle of light there is a total understanding of being, of the now, and of all that is. This really is the most precise way that we can refer to these things, would you not agree?

Consciousness

I began to see that there may be, within the orderly quality of the vibration, another quality which made a particular object what it was. Was a table aware in any sense of its structure? Was the act of creating anything imbuing that object with a consciousness through the act of creation? Was it only the property of the natural creative force of God or did man possess the ability to endow identity upon a man-made object?

G: Yes, yes. I think it comes back to the question of the way in which the particle has a separate existence and therefore within that existence, is there a consciousness that maintains that particle as a separate entity?

M: Yes.

G: Does an inanimate object also have consciousness?

M: Not if it is manufactured. Only if it is from something that has once lived. A tree sawn up and made into a table has a consciousness but a piece of plastic does not. Don't get the wrong idea regarding consciousness. You cannot injure or hurt the table. It does not have feeling; it cannot, deep within itself, cry out if it is kicked. That consciousness relates again to the energy field that surrounds it once it becomes a table. But it does have a vibration. If it were capable of changing that vibration – and it is not – you would not see it.

G: So if a table has consciousness, is that a form of intelligence that keeps its structure orderly?

M: We would agree with that. But the way we would put it is that it has the consciousness of the Creator that initially created what became a tree. The fact that it has changed some of its form to that of a table and is no longer experiencing life within the ground, does not alter the fact that it still experiences the same vibration as a tree. This does not change. If it did change, it would no longer exist in its present form.

G: *So the consciousness is actually of the form of the material of which it is made. So if it is made of wood, it still retains the idea or structure of wood?*

M: Indeed so.

G: *So does the person who made the table actually add anything to that consciousness, because it was a tree and it is now a different structure. Does the carpenter who made the table add something to the consciousness of that wood?*

M: He neither adds to, nor subtracts from. If you have a tree full of apples there is a certain consciousness within all of the apples. But they are all individual. If you take an apple and you eat it, you transform it into a different substance which is eventually evacuated from the body. That substance is then drawn into the Earth in the form it has become and that consciousness remains the same. But it simply changes the form, as it goes through the different processes. If you took the table and rendered it into sawdust it would still have the consciousness of the tree. It would simply have changed its format once more and become millions of tiny pieces that could be scattered. Within the part exists the whole.

G: *So if I understand correctly what you are saying, if we take an object like a tree and make it into a table, it still retains the consciousness of having been a tree. And if we then take the table and transform it into sawdust it still retains the consciousness of the tree because its molecular and chemical structure would, in fact, be the same blueprint as that of the tree. All that has happened is that it has been shaped and reduced into smaller particles, but it still retains that consciousness.*

Now, if in nuclear physics one changes the atomic structure, is that a means of changing the consciousness? Because if you take an atom of the tree and add a proton or neutron to it, it has now become a different substance (element). Is this a case of changing the consciousness?

M: You do not change the consciousness because what you add to it has its own consciousness. You are simply combining.

Consciousness and quantum theory

Now I try to link consciousness, as described by the Master, with the scientific idea of consciousness which is at the heart of quantum physics and which has proved so paradoxical, so unacceptable to scientists throughout the past 100 years. I wanted to know whether classical Newtonian physics was just a special or limiting case of the range of possibilities offered by quantum physics or were they different laws operating at different levels?

Laws of Physics

G: I understand that we experience life in the physical world, which can be described as the kinetic world, the world of physical objects in motion and the transfer of energy. But there is also an alternative model for creation, as science sees it. It's about the atomic structure, the electron, proton, the neutron, and family of sub-atomic particles about which science has made some discoveries. But these do not behave according to the kinetic laws like the Newtonian laws of motion. There must be a point where the atomic, quantum laws take over from the kinetic laws and I wonder what is the nature of that boundary? Where does one set of laws end and the other set of laws begin?

M: They are two separate laws. What science is not taking into consideration is that all things have existed forever and therefore what they are doing is working with particles that are constantly re-energizing themselves, rejuvenating themselves. They cannot cease to exist because they are part of existence. They might change their nature either by being added to something else or divided, but they cannot change the actual structure that they were first formulated into at the beginning of time – any more than you can change the nature of mankind, because he was engineered, you might say, to behave in a certain manner. He can become more aware; he can change as he becomes less primitive. As all things that surround him in and on his Earth accept these slight changes within his brain, within his ability to make greater use of what is there, as he uses his brain, he does, of course, grow more upright, lose the protective coat of hair because he learns to clothe himself.

All these different things which have come down through the hundreds of thousands of years have come down through consciousness being transmuted into intelligence – which again is within the mind of the Creator. These elements are used at different times, as they become applicable, most particularly as man becomes less primitive and more able to reason and argue with what he is doing. But it was there all the time. He is not creating anything himself; he is discovering what is there and, as he makes his experiments with nuclear fission, he is tapping into what has always been there for him to experiment upon since everything was first created.

As we have explained, even this is a misnomer because all things have always existed. What has been created is man. Everything else has always existed. Certain molecular changes took place after the Earth had gone through its time of being water, which, of course, provided the energy the Earth needed for all these many things to commence, to change, to become different, but it was largely man who aided and abetted this through his mind. Of course, individual man does not have an individual mind; he taps into the source. Source is mind. Man has brain, he uses it and when he moves into a state of higher consciousness, as it is called, he simply moves into the infinite.

How is our time with you, my son?

G: We only have five minutes left.

M: So how do you wish to use that five minutes? Do you wish to sum up what you feel we have shared with you, or have you another question that is quite speedy?

G: I think a summing-up would be appropriate.

M: Then go ahead, my son.

G: Everything that is has always existed and it is consciousness that gives everything its structure and its form, as long as that form has come from a natural source, such as a tree.

M: And what name would you give to the consciousness?

G: I would think that the consciousness is an intelligence that is like the blueprint of the atomic and the molecular structure.

M: The consciousness at source is God. Otherwise you are correct because there are permutations, mutations and so forth.

G: *There are laws that govern our existence in the physical world, but there is also the quantum world. That subatomic world exists alongside our physical world and therefore both laws apply simultaneously. The structure of matter comes from source, from God, as we know it.*

M: Good. Now our time is up, so until the next meeting, farewell. Shalom.

G: *Farewell, Master. Shalom.*

Chapter 3

Conversation Two

Spheres of light. A further definition of consciousness. Quantum theory. Mathematics. Parallel universes. Black holes. Near-death experiences.

M: Greetings, my son. Shalom.

G: Welcome, Master. Shalom.

The Master and I began by discussing the general shape of the book. He wanted to know if I planned to include teachings regarding the nature of life on other planets, because this was very important. I have always taken a very open view regarding life on other planets and have no problem with the concept that what the Master refers to as 'planetary beings' might visit Earth from time to time.

M: We are well aware that there is much controversy as to whether human life is replicated on any of the known planets. We have been quite explicit in our reply regarding this, by emphasizing that the life forms that are in different planets are forms that cannot, at the present time, be recognized through anything of a scientific nature. At some time, possibly, the instruments and the calculations, as well as the advanced forms of radio communication which are taking place in the scientific world, might very well be able to pick up signals from the planets. But at the present time this is not available, so it would be to the advantage of the reader to be aware that there are life forms there and they are extremely advanced forms of life.

G: I certainly think that it is a very important point, and one that I would consider fairly essential to include.

Spheres of light
This concept might need some explanation, as I, for one, had never encountered this before. The Master teaches that the Earth is a sphere of matter upon which we reside and surrounding the physical planet are the spiritual spheres where we have a soul existence. Each of the spiritual spheres exists at a different vibrational frequency. I imagine

it to be something like a radio dial; all stations exist concurrently at their designated frequency but the tuner is set to receive only one of them at any given time. So it is with the spirit spheres, of which there are seven levels around the Earth. The Master refers to them as bands of colour because that is the way that he sees them. For more detail see Appendix I at the back of the book.

M: There is also the relationship with the spheres of light, which has not been picked up in any concrete way by science, although we have it on excellent authority that groups of scientists have been made aware of electrical impulses that they cannot explain, which encircle the world. Some with their instruments have been aware of the colours that encircle the Earth; astronauts also confirmed this when they have been orbiting the Earth in their machines. But scientists have not actually established what the different responses, radio responses, relate to or whether any form of life can be associated with them. We have again discussed these things at different times, but have not truly related the spirit world and the soul to anything comparable in the other spheres, or upon the Earth itself. This might well form a suitable topic with us on some occasion [see Chapter 6].

G: *Yes, I feel it fits very neatly into the concept of the book.*

M: Indeed so.

The Master further defines consciousness
Scientists attempt to describe in intellectual terms what they mean by consciousness and it features very largely in some of the interpretations in quantum theory, for instance. However, no one has yet defined absolutely what consciousness is and how it may be measured so I decided to ask the Master for his definition of this elusive quality.

G: *It would appear that man has very little understanding of what consciousness is. We use the term but we really don't understand the concept. Could you give me a definition of what you understand as consciousness?*

M: Consciousness is the connection between the creation of the unseen and the creation of the seen as it applies to man. This also applies to all the rest of the living world, the animal world and even the harmony that exists between plant life, tree life, shrubs and so forth. They have their own consciousness, their own sense of reality, of the earth beneath and its nourishment, the sky above and that which surrounds them, totally at ease, totally aware, even though there is no great mind or thought behind them. For humanity, even when there is no active thought process, just absorbing the energy of living – that is the consciousness of man.

A greater awareness, a greater consideration of all of life can be obtained through the many ways of absorbing the God force within, to open the mind, to open the resources that man has for this awareness. But actual consciousness is only present during the earthly life. It is a very different appraisal when the soul is absent and has returned to spirit.

G: I presume then that the consciousness expands into a higher awareness because you are then free from the limitations of the physiology and of the brain.

M: Indeed, the mind is of the soul but the brain is of the body. That could answer a question that science has been putting for generations of time.

G: I have this picture of the mind and of the brain. It is like a child holding a large balloon; basically the mind is the volume of the balloon, and the brain is like the little thin cord that attaches it to the hand of the child. It's almost as if the limitations of one's experience of the mind are actually because of the limitations of the cord that binds it.

M: Very good, yes, that would be a good description. The mind within man could not exist if the brain is absent or has died. In the case of a person who is about to die or perhaps is brain-dead and many people would say, 'What kind of consciousness of what is taking place around them do they have? Do they hear? Are they frantic within their inert body?' The answer is no, they are not present, the body itself is still functioning on the autonomic level, still breathing, the blood is still moving through the heart, through the veins, the organs within are still being nourished, but the mind is not present because the brain no longer functions. So without the mind there can be no awareness of what is taking place around them. Virtually they are already in spirit, like the outer precinct or lobby of the great vision that they are about to enter, preparing to be accepted, preparing to see again the souls of the loved ones that have gone before.

G: *So does the mind have a physical location in the brain?*

M: No.

G: *No, but the presence of the brain establishes the mind within the consciousness?*

M: That is so. You are not aware of the oxygen within the air that you breathe, are you?

G: No.

M: But it is there.

G: *Yes, when you think about breathing, it is a great act of trust, isn't it, that you breathe out expecting –*

M: – to breathe in the correct mixtures.

G: *Yes.*

M: Exactly. As the brain connects with the mind, the vale of the mind, and brings about memory and connects with those parts of the brain which relate to memory, so they work together almost automatically. But the greater expansion of the mind and the awareness of thought and memory and visualization depends a very great deal on the capacity of the individual to accept the spiritual within life. Those that are dead to anything other than the material world in which they live have very little to do with their minds and the consciousness of the life that lies ahead.

Quantum theory and mysticism
I have been looking at the nature of matter from the scientific viewpoint and also from the perspective of the teach-

ings of the Master. The Master tells us that the creative aspect of God is an energy, a vibration, an intelligence from which all the material or spatial universe forms.

I am also aware of such Zen concepts as 'hearing the sound of one hand clapping'. To our rational mind this makes no sense at all. But if you take your attention to the quantum reality then the coming together of matter and antimatter produces vibration (light and radiation). The analogy could be applied to a physical hand clapping an unmanifest hand in the realm of spirit (or antimatter) producing sound, which is also a vibration. Following on from this speculation I wonder whether the mystics and enlightened ones can, at will, perceive and experience the world at the quantum level. I find the underlying quantum reality a very mysterious basis for the deterministic world of classical, or Newtonian, physics.

One of the most famous answers to this Zen koan was 'Mu', which in Japanese means 'no thing'. By giving this answer the monk is understood to have indicated to his master that he had transcended the world of duality and penetrated the mind of God, which is brimming over with the potential of all things but in which no thing exists. The mind of God is essentially a paradox, full and empty at the same time. Thus from the apparent void of space, matter and antimatter has the potential to be created.

Quantum theory and the effect of the observer

G: I am trying to look for a link between the quantum world and the world of classical physics. What is the relationship of these two paradoxical realities?

M: In trying to find the factor that links these things, science should really look toward the principal of acceptance and belief, rather than always relying on the mathematical fact. The universe and its creation were spiritual concepts of God. It was not considered that it should be verifiable on the scientific levels of proven fact, with all things taking place in a way that must be acceptable mathematically. The universe and its creation can be acceptable on a spiritual level within the mind and within the feelings of man, irrespective of his intellectual judgements regarding the rights and wrongs of all activities.

There is among our channel's photographic experiments a

photograph that she took of a sunset and this shows in such minute detail the components of light. It is probably unique because normally photographing light in this way would not produce a negative. Now in some ways we are able to influence these things by our own intervention, which is independent of the material world. These things can be changed depending upon who is doing the experiment, and how their minds relate to our concept of truth. There has to be a complete link before our influence can have an effect on the material world. So we would like you to pursue that because it shows in such minute detail these things that you have just presented to us and the way they relate, so will you do this, my son? We feel it will answer much.

G: Yes, I will.

M: In various parts of the book, and also in other volumes that we have been instrumental in channelling, we make reference to the spiral of life, that it is in every concept of being. It is within thought as well as within the genetic pattern which is one of those things that science has now brought forward for man to investigate and accept: that scientists have actually looked within the DNA of all the species and discovered that they replicate through the spiral.

In capturing the essence within the sunset in the way that the camera did, it illustrated these different forms of spiral that exist which are all on their way, as it were, to fulfilling the function that they have been born to express. The vast energy of the Sun is the most powerful energy that exists outside the bowels of the Earth, because deep within it there is the compensating energy that also maintains the Earth in its position in respect to the other planets, the Sun and the Moon. You could say, within that vast energy of the Sun is the birthplace of man's universe, for all the energy that feeds him throughout his existence over millions of years. All those little varying spirals with their colours, their lengths, their smallness or largeness, they have all been born and they are all hastening toward that function in exactly the same way as within the body the spirals of DNA go to make a limb or an organ.

So you can call that moment caught on the photograph the incubation, the womb of life depositing for mankind everything that he needs for his growth and to maintain life. That is encapsulated in that particular moment of movement, that particular fraction of a second which has been captured in time.

There are also other things, of course there are, within that picture. There are certain things which have been born which are not needed so much, that are perhaps imperfect. Nature isn't perfect, in fact it is very imperfect, and there are things within nature born to die immediately because they have no useful function. The difference between nature and man's concept of it is that nothing is wasted. Even that which dies has its purpose. Therefore within that picture that you have, you can see the death of something as it is moving through all the living spirals.

G: That's very good, Master. Thank you. That really has illuminated this picture for me.

Mathematics

It has always seemed to me that physics is our culture's attempt to rationalize the physical world we see and experience around us using logic and repeatable experimentation and observation. The language that physics uses to express its theories is mathematics whereas in the past, great civilizations have often used mystical and philosophical approaches to gain knowledge. The psychic and spiritual development of an individual allow him to gain great insight into the subtle aspects of creation. In our culture, reluctantly at first, with great opposition from religious authority, science was born using the human intellect, logic and empirical method, which have today produced the technological and medical advantages we currently enjoy.

G: Your comment about mathematics ... I've always considered that mathematics was rather like the language of God. When physicists, particularly in the early part of this century, were investigating the building blocks of nature, they used mathematics in order to clothe the abstract ideas that they were working with. Mathematics allowed them to make predictions that could be experimented with, to prove whether the ideas were correct or not. Now from your comment, I infer that belief is necessary also, and that the mind of the experimenter has an influence on the outcome of the experiment.

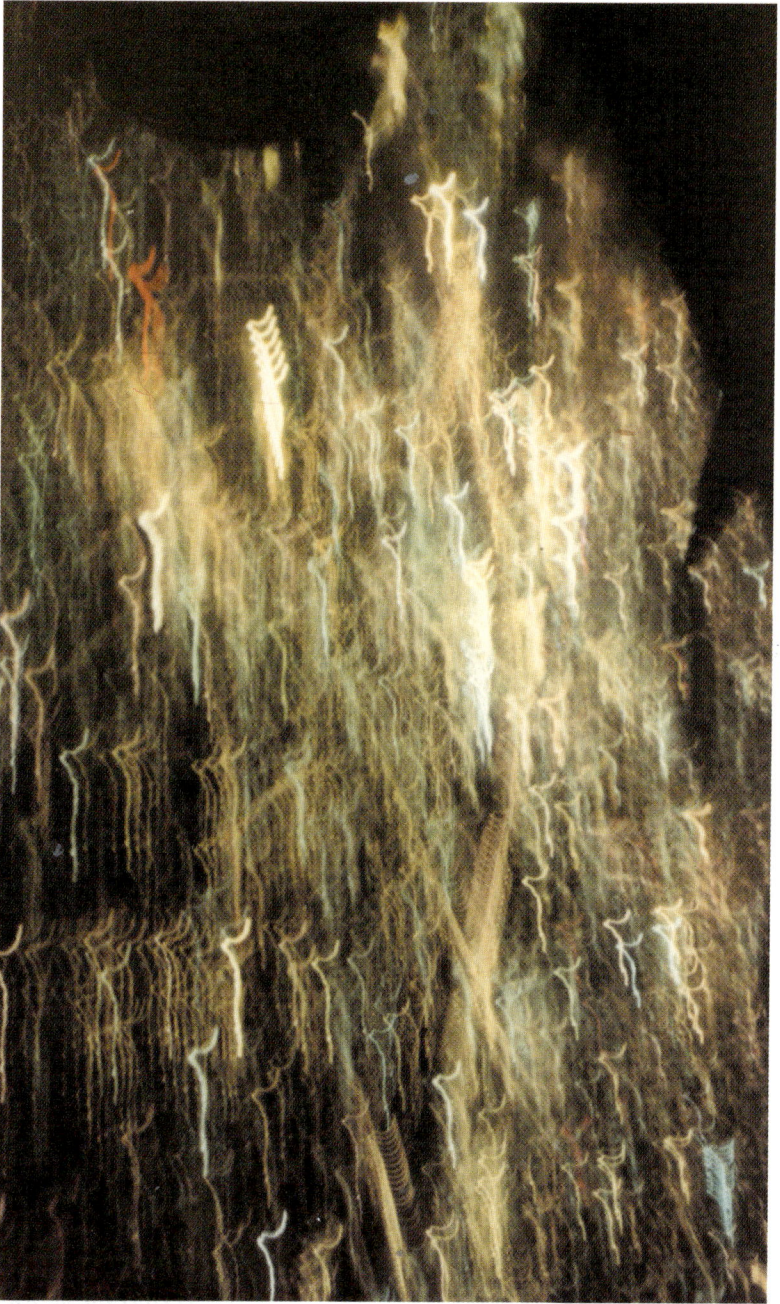

This photograph is reminiscent of the photographic traces produced when atoms are smashed in accelerators to produce the sub-atomic particles.

M: Indeed so.

G: So does that mean that mathematics does not provide as complete a description of the nature of reality as physicists and mathematicians would expect?

M: That is true. Scientists always leave inspiration out of the equation. They do not take this into account at all because of the requirement that everything must be repeatable. They do not accept that what they are inspired to investigate can sometimes produce results because of the way they are approaching it which could not be reproduced by another scientist, or even by themselves under different circumstances. Going back to that photo, we doubt if it could ever be produced again even with the same camera and a similar sunset. Probably all that would be achieved would be blackness. But because everything was correct for the experiment to take place, and the different modulations within the mind were correct for acceptance, in the belief that this could indeed take place, it did so. It is like a medium who has a firm belief that they can draw to them an aspect of spirit life which will clothe itself in a recognisable form, and this will indeed be present with them. Whereas other mediums, or channellers, who do not believe in this form of experience, can never achieve it.

G: In quantum theory there is the concept that also states that the consciousness and mindset of the experimenter influences the results and I think it is a rather abstract concept for scientists to fully understand. They need that repeatability and it seems to me, from what you're saying, that repeatability is, in itself, not possible because you never recreate the exact circumstances of an experiment, particularly on the subtle levels.

M: Exactly so, and also, it is the mind itself which has never been, and never can be, analysed because it stems from the thought within God. As God is an interaction of all the essences within the universe itself, and as God is within the most minute form of energy in all its concepts, and that in itself is of the mind, it cannot be analysed, it cannot be repeated. A thought cannot be repeated in exactly the same way. There is always change taking place which makes the thought either greater or lesser with each repeat of the same value. So when scientists are endeavouring to repeat certain scientific experiments it cannot always be done, and until this is accepted by them, they will not go further forward into certain beliefs and facts. Are we making ourselves clear, my son?

Thought

G: Yes, you are, Master. I feel instinctively that that is the case. Without realizing it then, some years ago, I came to a point where I realized that the mind, or the consciousness of the person concerned, had much greater access to truth than mathematics, scientific knowledge, and experimentation.

M: Exactly. If you work on the principle that thought cannot be caught and isolated, it cannot be interrupted in its motion, and that motion isolated, and repeated, then you're getting very near to the truth of man's mind and of the universal ability or potential for total change which is taking place all the time.

Scientists have recently discovered that they can go back much further into what they consider to be the beginning of the universe than they could even a year or two ago. But having accepted that they can go back to that particular point, they are then immobilized from going back any further until man's mind can release sufficient intuition and inspiration to find that next fact and explore it. If they had more imagination, and if they related more to what they have already discovered and can prove – especially with the help of the computer systems now available – if they could lock into that and then make an inspirational leap backwards, they would probably find that they are very near to the truth of it. But what they seem unable to do is to relate their facts to what is taking place in each age, as there are infinitesimal changes, all the time, within the universe. If there were not, how would man's intellect continue to improve, making him able to accept what is taking place in life now, which he could not do a million years ago?

There has to be a collective change to encourage the intellect and the mind to move forward in this acceptance, and that which is taking place within the neutrons and the protons, and all the rest of the terminology that describes space, matter, antimatter, and everything else that they are studying. Those infinitesimal changes cannot be noted mathematically, because they cannot be photographed, nor seen by the naked eye. It is all theorizing upon what they consider is there, but they cannot see it. They can only see the reactions related to it.

G: So for the progress of science, I think what you are saying is that we are not going to make an intellectual leap. It's going to be an intuitive or inspirational leap that requires as its basis a change in the core beliefs of man.

M: That describes it very accurately.

Collective consciousness
G: So is there a collective mindset? Is it a case that mankind in general holds back those gifted individuals who can see slightly further, until the basic level of belief rises?

M: You could put it that way, because man is on so many different levels of understanding and intellect according to his background and even the background of his continent, of his country. There are certain areas within the world that can never catch up with the rest because the knowledge is simply not made available to them.

So the intellect is far behind in some areas, in the same way as in space itself, in the universe, there is not a collective understanding of the progress that is surrounding all the planetary life, including the Earth. It is in stages from the first belief, the first thought, that process of experimentation which then led further and further forward until the planets were created. Then the availability of all the products that came about from that invention, you might call it, which allowed the Earth, far more advanced than any other planet, to be created – the concept of the Earth, and the concept of the other planetary life being quite different.

However, that was a slow process forward, and intuition, imagination, inspiration took place within the mind of the Creator. So all these processes fell into place like a giant jigsaw puzzle. The concept was there, but then it was how to create everything within that concept, to make it reality. So you can see that it is not possible to relate everything to one small atom and expect it simply to grow from that point because each point, each conception, was different in some regard.

How parallel universes are created
The idea that parallel universes form whenever there is a

decision point reached on a subatomic level has intrigued scientists and science-fiction writers alike. The theories spring from the statistical nature of the universe at the quantum level where, at its simplest, the concept would suggest that, for instance, if an electron has a finite probability that it can be in one of two places then a parallel universe opens up to contain each of the eventualities. In this case two universes would be created.

Multiplying this across all the atoms and other particles in the universe would involve a staggering number of parallel universes, each spawning a vast array of others in turn as time moves forward. This would also imply that we concurrently exist in a vast number of universes, whereas we appear to be only aware of one. This fundamental paradox puzzles me.

Hitherto, my concept, and very simple understanding, of a parallel universe was that if I decide to go down to the end of the road and there is a left turn and a right turn and I take the left turn, there is another universe created where I take the right turn. Under those circumstances, when I think of every decision I've made throughout my life, that would add up to a very large number of parallel universes. I had also not appreciated that parallel universes open up on a global level, based on collective universal consciousness created by the free will of mankind, and not on an individual level of consciousness.

The Master also makes reference to parallel universes in his teachings and I wondered at the mechanism whereby the parallel universes that the Master speaks of come into being and whether it is our minds, the exercise of our free will, that create these alternative realities or whether it is part of a larger, more cosmic process. I had mistakenly understood that parallel universes were created in pairs, a positive and a negative. I further assumed that one would relate to matter and the other to antimatter.

Parallel universes

G: *Now, we talk of the mind, and one of the questions I have here is about parallel universes. Is the creation of a parallel universe a creation of the mind or of God?*

M: Of God. There is actually more than one Earth, more than

one place of residence for man. Again the positive and negative influences that man has created throughout his life create that which he does, the progress he is making throughout the aeons of time. As he returns to the spheres, this becomes a positive energy from which he can recreate an atom of himself and it can go to one parallel universe or the other. So that some of the concepts within the Higher Self can choose one reality, while the soul can reproduce a more positive aspect of that life in another reality, the two often converging, overlapping and even exchanging awareness within those lives.

Black holes
Since it was discovered by scientists that the universe that we interact with is only about 1% of the total and that the other 99% is what is called 'dark matter' which is material that we cannot detect by any known means, then the search has been on to find physical evidence for this. Black holes are very dense objects, so dense in fact that the gravitational field is enormous. This immense gravitational field pulls in all objects in its vicinity. Whole planetary systems, and indeed whole galaxies, may be swallowed up by the small dense object. It is so dense that even light is pulled in and cannot escape its influence – hence the expression 'black hole'. In the region of a black hole time and space distort and an effect is created of a tunnel or wormhole where time and space cease to exist in the form that we know and experience it.

G: What I gather from what you are saying is that there are, in fact, two universes, a positive and a negative. Is the meeting point of those two universes something like a black hole?

M: The short answer to that is yes. For simplicity's sake, if it were indeed possible to be drawn into the black hole and survive, the parallel universe would be entered as you emerged on the other side.

G: Presumably, on the other side of that black hole, matter would also be drawn in?

M: There is no sense of time, for a start. There is no movement, there is no actual taking place of activity. It is all on a mind scale. It is occurring, and yet not occurring, so you could say that it is simply being. There is a transmission of energy that can separate the positive and negative of what man thinks is occurring, and creates that reality from it. You see that black hole as something that is turning like a spiral, within thought, because thought must have a function to relate to. Thought cannot accept inactivity, and non-movement of energy, or matter. The mind is an overactive creation and therefore despite attempts to silence it, to encourage it to remain immobile, it will still continue to interact with all things that surround it. It will still interact with all other thought, all other minds, which in turn all interact with the mind of God. So if you try and note that process and relate it to the entry of a black hole, as the entry is made it is already complete in its negative aspect.

Meditation and black holes

G: So at the point of separation between the positive and negative within a black hole, would that point be the still point of meditation when you go beyond the active mind?

M: The point of silence, as it is quite beautifully supposed to be. But few, if any, have ever actually reached it. They can anticipate that moment of absolute silence, but it does not exist, therefore it cannot be emulated.

G: The picture I'm getting is that the universes really emerged from that black hole into positive and negative creation. Would it be right to say that the centre of that is where God is?

M: It would. God is indeed that silence within the self that man cannot visualize in any way other than as himself. Those who are still ignorant in this concept must relate to a figure, or to a point of infinitesimal light. Man thinks there is either light or darkness and that which is good relates to the light and that which is not relates to the darkness. But if you put both together, overlapping each other, what do you produce?

G: I would think that you produce this stillness, and you would transcend the duality of existence.

M: But how do you prove that theory? Could you prove it either mathematically or scientifically?

G: *I think you could only prove the concept by analogy. For instance, you might take the coming together of a positron and an electron to amalgamate and produce light as your premise. If you have the concept that God is energy, then you could say this is a scientific parallel to the process of matter and antimatter coming together to produce a God vibration. But there is no way that you would definitely be able to produce the mathematics to prove the existence of God. It may be possible through a mind experiment but you would have to believe in it sufficiently in order to get your mind into the correct vibration to experience that concept.*

Near-death experiences

M: And that, of course, is not possible in life. It is possible in death, because the mind is then totally limitless. But in the confines of a physical body, the mind relating through the brain has its limitations. There is one way that many people experience this travelling through the universe while still in the body. That is when they have this near-death experience that is being spoken of so greatly, because at that moment the consciousness is aware of separation. In sleep it is not aware of this. It takes place but it is masked by the dream state, or conversely by the depth of sleep which removes all thought, all brain activity. As, of course, does anaesthesia, where there is no brain activity that is recorded through the mind's sensor. So when people return to consciousness they are neither aware of going into unconsciousness, nor of what is occurring during that time until they awaken. It is as one fraction of a second of time between the two actions.

Now, in a near-death experience the first thing that occurs, in the majority of cases, is this feeling of rushing through space. Some have even recorded being aware of a tunnel ahead of them, full of white light, and the sound of rushing wind as something hurtles at tremendous speed through this tunnel. You can relate that, if you desire, to the black hole, because you are going from one universe to another in order to experience what is taking place at exactly the same time as in your own universe. But because it has a much higher vibration than your universe, it can only be experienced through unconsciousness that is not just near-death but actual death, the release of the soul and its tremendous movement as it seeks to return to the universe to which it is attached.

It would appear, from what the Master is saying, that a parralel universe is a state of consciousness. Another way of saying this is that a person may have an etheric presence in all parallel universes that exist, but that materially he is tuned to this reality. He might occasionally experience life in another parallel universe, but only in the dream state.

The only way that man can refer to this is through the silver cord which keeps the soul within the body. There isn't a physical cord, but at one time it was noted that the umbilical cord which is attached to the child is a very similar kind of cord to that which attaches the soul to the body when it is exploring its spiritual self during the time of sleep. Etherically the cord has to remain attached to the body to animate it, to keep it alive because, although it is sleeping, it cannot be devoid of the soul because when the soul leaves in death the body immediately begins to decompose and to become unnecessary to the life of the soul. So there is a metaphysical linking during sleep and during spirit exploration. Many different beliefs talk about severing the cord when the soul is released. That metaphysical attachment which the soul has to the physical no longer remains constant when the soul is released in death.

The soul is not within the body. It never has been, it never will be. The body relates to the soul, and if the soul removes itself from the mind and brain within the body, then the body can no longer exist. To many people we refer to the soul being within every cell of the body, but that is for simplicity, that is to allow those who can only relate to a fact to be able to relate to our calculations and to our surmise, so that they can understand more greatly what we are talking about. But in reality it is not in the material body; it cannot be so because the soul is not material, it is not matter, and it cannot relate to matter. The soul remains in a parallel universe of its own, which, of course, we will talk about, my son, at some future time.

G: *And now, our time is up, Master.*

M: It is all too soon, is it not, my son? So we will say farewell. Shalom.

Chapter 4

Conversation Three

The creation of parallel universes. The Eldars. Parallel universes and the mind. Influencing our environment. Earth-healing meditation. Time and spirals. The three aspects of God.

M: Welcome again, my son. Shalom.

G: Welcome, Master. Shalom.

Parallel universes

After our last talk I was still very puzzled by the concepts described as parallel universes and how they link with black holes. It seems to me that there are different kinds of parallel universes. Some are the spirit spheres surrounding the planets, seven for the Earth and three for other planets. There are also parallel worlds created by the exercise of the free will given to mankind. These operate according to the events which take place on Earth.

It is rather like one scenario propounded by quantum physics where the whole gamut of possibilities exist until the experimenter observes the result. At this point all other possible results then fade away from this reality. There is a theory that a parallel universe opens up to accommodate each of all the possible results of the experiment. I'm not sure I can quite get my mind around that concept as it would mean that there would be by now millions of replicas of the Earth for every decision that has been made.

Parallel universes. Time and space

G: From our previous talks, the fundamental points that I have noted down are these: when two parallel universes are overlaid, transcendence is the result. We were talking about black holes and parallel universes, with matter and antimatter coming together and the still point in the centre being where God is. You then went on to say that to experience it, it is necessary for the soul to separate from the body, as in a near-death experience. You were at great pains to point out the soul is not actually in the body but independent from it.

There is an interesting statement that you made about the soul: the soul remains in a parallel universe of its own. Now, I've got a question about that. Does that mean that when you have two parallel universes with the black hole as the transition point, is there a corresponding set of parallel spiritual spheres?

M: Yes, that is the case.

The etheric that surrounds the human self is the soul essence of humanity, and therefore the spiritual realms that surround the Earth are also of an etheric nature. That is why they are not immediately apparent from space. The outline around the world can be ascertained from a space vehicle, in the same way as those who are attuned to looking at the aura of human beings can see this faint whiteness which initially surrounds the body, and if they are really well attuned they would also be able to see the colours which emanate.

G: *There is a final point: is there just the one black hole in the universe or are there several?*

M: There are several, because there is more than one universe.

G: *If there are parallel universes on either side of each black hole, are they the same universes on each side? Do all the black holes lead to the same parallel or do they lead to different universes?*

M: They lead to different ones.

How are the universes created?
At this point I was still finding this very difficult and was trying to understand the experience of being in a parallel universe. I hold fast to my concept of the radio dial as it seems to me that everything is just vibration and we use our mind to tune into different realities. Because we are not consciously aware of these possibilities, most of us remain ignorant of the power of the mind.

G: *What is the mechanism whereby parallel universes exist? Do they, for instance, occupy the same space as our universe and are just on a different frequency, or are they in a different physical dimension?*

M: They occupy the same space, if you assume that there is space.

G: Yes, it does bring us on to the nature of space and time. What I was thinking of particularly was when we were discussing matter and antimatter. For experimentation to have been done on that, my line of thinking was that if you have matter and antimatter coming together in these very subtle areas of physics, then the anti-matter must have come from the other side of the parallel universe divide. In order for it to manifest itself on this side, presumably the energy transfer would have been equal and opposite across that boundary. So that as a piece of matter from the parallel universe manifests itself in this universe, this dimension, an exchange of energy must have gone across to the other side. Is that reasoning correct?

M: We follow you completely, but we are thinking of the way to describe what takes place with as equal a lucidity as your remarks toward us. Let us take an example: if circumstances occur that you enter a parallel universe and become aware in your physical body during the waking state that you have crossed the boundary. What you're saying is, what is there in your own universe to compensate for the absence, is this so?

Crossing the divide
G: Yes.

M: There is nothing there to represent yourself. You are absent. Those people who might miss you, wonder where you are and be searching for you, would, of course, do so in vain – unless they come to exactly the same circumstances where the frequencies between the universes coincide, which does not occur very often.

It does occur with the soul body during the time of sleep. Very often, particularly lucid dreams will be so because you have entered a different timescale or a different universe during that period of time. The soul has indeed manifested with its cloak of personality, either a few years before the present time, or many years into the future – or even across the divide itself and has awareness of the continuity of life from some past experience. To elucidate on this: when there have been experiences early in life that have changed direction, it can possibly be because the parallel universe has allowed the awakening of purpose to take place within its precincts. The personality has greater awareness of what is taking place there than in the present time. This could help the personality to shed the past, and the ultimate results of the past, to go in a different direction, to begin a different path.

Occasionally, if somebody truly does vanish, if somebody walks out of the house and never returns, or even returns many years hence, it can be that these universes have reached a frequency which is the same [synchronicity]. Therefore the personality has crossed over. It may be many years later when it crosses back, unaware of what has taken place in the interim, and the person would appear to have a clouded memory, or suffered a brainstorm, a loss of memory, whatever explanation has been given. This happens quite frequently but usually it is less dramatic. There is an awareness that a change must take place. The personality follows the different path and the etheric personality from that life continues in the parallel existence. Is this very confusing? Can we help you by putting it differently?

G: I am certainly a little puzzled by the parallel universes. Is there a mapping of one parallel to another? For instance, is there my composite already existing in that parallel universe?

M: The short answer is yes.

G: And is what shifts between my personality in this universe and another universe my soul, or would it be my personality that would cross the divide?

M: It is the soul that actually crosses the divide, but it is recognized by the present personality. When it is rediscovered, say in a dream state ... We have thought of a comparison that might help understanding.

The Eldars
The Master teaches that the Eldars, or Els, were the first beings to inhabit the Earth. They were part spirit, part human and were known in the Bible as the Elohim, the multitude of God.

Dinosaurs and parallel universes. Astral travelling
In a fairly recent teaching, in answer to a question, we explained that the lives of the Eldars of some millions of years ago, the lives of the dinosaurs, and similar animals of many millions of

years ago, still exist. They have vanished from planet Earth within this present universe that surrounds it, but everything was not killed quite in the way that science believes and which some scientists feel they have proved. There was a massive shifting of energy at the time. When the great catastrophe occurred many animals were, of course, killed, but many also shifted into a parallel universe where they still continue to have life. They have evolved in the same way as humanity, changing their form, their understanding, having become less cumbersome within their more present lives. If there were to be a shift back into the present universe, they would then be seen as a different form of animal life, different livestock, you could say.

The same with the Eldars; their lives continue in a different universe. A different replica of what was taking place at that time still exists for them, but with even greater intelligence, greater ability to teach, to share, and to bring humanity into alignment with the spiritual concepts.

So it is the same thing taking place, on an hourly, daily basis within your world, as these parallels cross and interweave their patterns together and as the soul, in its etheric self, during the sleep state, passes to and fro into these lives. It is possible to feel that you are yourself walking streets of the past, or being aware of what seems to be a very futuristic life going on around you. It is just cast aside as being the ramblings of the mind during sleep. But there should be more interrogation and investigation into these forms of dreams. They are so very vivid; they do not just vanish as the great majority of dreams do upon waking. They are often vivid with colour; there is a feeling within the body of activity, of things taking place. The body feels pain if it is attacked, or if it is lifted into the air or dropped. There is a resultant awareness in your personality, as it lies asleep in your bed. The soul itself is floating apart from the body, which is why it has awareness of what is taking place. Does this make it clearer?

Parallel universes and the mind of man
G: Yes, it does make it a little clearer. We tend to think of time as being essentially linear, the fourth dimension that we move through, this sea of time in which change occurs. Could it be that time is just a way of shifting gradually from one frequency to another, in terms of the parallel universes, rather like moving the tuner along a radio dial to pick up different stations? So could it

be that in fact the future already exists in a parallel universe, as does the past?

M: Changes are already in existence. Humanity comes into these changes as and when he is prepared so to do. Change does not come about solely through man's intention. Inventions, when they are discovered, come about at a time when it is opportune, when all other energies have combined to make that result applicable to man's understanding and the level of intelligence that he has reached throughout his existence which make those inventions acceptable to him. They were in existence, time-wise, one thousand years ago. There could then have been aeroplanes that came into the sky and went from one place to another but man's comprehension, his state of evolution, could not accept this. He could not even be truly aware of it, even in his dream state. If he were, he would consider himself to be hallucinating. But as the time came nearer to when it was applicable to have these items in space that carried man, then he permitted his ideas to confirm what he had visualized. All other matters that would assist him with this then came about so that the inventions slowly appeared over time.

When we say that time only exists in man's concept, this is why. If all things were applicable, all at the same time, it would then render the universe that surrounds you to one atom, one minute part of an atom that exists and then dematerializes. Because this cannot be so, because there has to be continuity and an acceptable reason for existence, it is allowed to expand and grow. The atom constantly reforms itself so that man's mind and his brain can accept what is taking place around him. The parallel universes allow the growth to become that much greater. As one universe appears to have a greater intelligence guiding it, so another can still move more slowly, can understand more greatly what is occurring, even to a point of the enjoyment of certain activities. When these are expounded upon, and are no longer necessary, then the point of contact and reversal can take place so that the next movement forward of discovery can occur.

All the time it is as though man is moving through a kaleidoscope of visual energies that he can relate to as he expands and grows within his consciousness, as his soul moves him forward to the next step. Which is why sometimes a scientist is apparently so much in advance of others that are working on the same technique. One may perhaps find a cure for AIDS, another will dispute this, will demand the years of experimentation, of testing, of making quite sure that there is an actual cure for this virus. But the one who has moved into the space of finding that cure will disparage the slowness, the plodding of his companion as he holds back the whole project because he is not yet ready for this expansion of knowledge. Are you getting a clearer picture?

Preparation for world events
G: *Yes, I think I am. I think what you are saying is that it is the understanding and the belief system of man that determine how far forward and how fast progress can proceed.*

M: That is so, but it is the soul that propels it forward, possibly at a faster pace, in order that more can be achieved in a certain span of time. Where there are certain events taking place – let us take the episodes that led to the last world war, for example. Science had to speed up, realizing that if war came, it was not likely to be the war of the hand-to-hand combat, of the soldiers sitting in their trenches throwing infantile weapons at each other; they realized that there would be far greater disasters that would have to be combated.

Prior to the war, millions of male children had been conceived and born, as the spiritual forces were very well aware that, otherwise, with the normal genetic increase, virtually all males within the world would be annihilated due to the kind of war that spirit and the Higher Selves knew was going to take place. This illustrates that much of the future must already be anticipated, so that other progress can take place, through the disaster and beyond it. So nature prepared for this (you can call it nature, instead of spirit if you wish). Nature brought into life all these male children.

Most of them were conceived just after the first world war, and millions more came into life after the second, – hopefully not to be relegated once more beneath the soil, but to be able to take part in such wonderful experiences and growth patterns as the Golden Age, when so many more will then be needed, not for devastation, not for death, but to be able to grow and expand their consciousness into the spiritual existence which is contained within the Golden Age. It is already here, and a lot of our teaching is showing that man is moving into what is already prepared for him, and encouraging both the spiritual awareness, and the manifestation of knowledge, the intelligence within the brain, to be able to visualize and to enjoy.

Influencing our environment
The mind is a most powerful influence on our individual lives. There is a growing awareness of the mind and body connection and a realization that our feelings, our state of being, our attitude of mind influence our health, outlook, progress and experience of life. But as I began to understand from the Master's words, the collective mind also influences the condition of life on Earth, our society and culture, ethics and progress, our knowledge and beliefs, the leaders we choose, and the health of the planet. Realizing this can enable us to correct the imbalances in our lives and to create social, commercial, and environmental structures which serve mankind and the planet, and do not seek to subjugate or enslave.

The power of visualization.
G: So there is a lot of wisdom in a statement such as 'Follow your dreams', because that is the way the soul makes manifest its intention for the future?

M: That is very much so, but also, what else is it that scientists do? They mix a few components into a glass tube, and they see certain reactions, and that triggers within themselves a reaction. They feel that it is not just those components showing them something that happens through the mixture that is taking place; they have a vision of what it can be used for, or what moves beyond that actual action and then into something much greater than that.

So also do visionaries. They do not compound their physics, their mathematics; they work with their dreams. They work with what they wish to be part of. They have a visualization of Utopia, of the promised land, and in their own way, through their own efforts, they move forward to receive it. But during that movement forward, during the visualization, which they hope and pray will manifest, they speak of it to others, and in that speaking the mind is alerted to that vision. As more and more dwell within that vision so the vision opens, they move into it, and it becomes a reality.

Earth-healing meditation

One important application of the power of the mind and its ability to visualize is in Earth-healing meditations. The Master has invited those who wish to take part in this process at the times of the full and new moon to visualize golden light entering in a spiral through themselves and into the Earth, replenishing its crystalline centre and bringing harmony, regeneration and balance to the mineral, plant, animal and human life on the planet. For more details on how to do this, see Appendix II.

G: So it is very important that man has a vision in order to move forward in a structured way, which is not harmful to himself, or to the planet?

M: It is crucial. It is also shown when we request such simple things as the focus of light going into an imaginary centre of the world. Who can really equate what is taking place in the Earth's centre with what is imagined or even what scientists have predicted as being so? It is the vision within those people, of feeling that light, through their instigation, is travelling toward this important centre which needs restoring and which needs to be filled again with all that has been extracted from it. It is pure visualization, pure imagination, and yet it becomes fact because the very vision brings about the action, because the action is there waiting to be moved into.

Everything is there, my son, the end of the world, the completion of the universe, it has already happened. In the same way that science is now going further and further back, to the creation, to the first moment of life within the universe. When man reaches that point, he will have reached the last moment of existence.

G: So the whole cycle is from the unmanifest to the manifest, and back to the unmanifest?

M: Indeed so.

Dimensions

The Master says that time and space are the same energy which, from a scientific point of view, might seem to be strange to us as we do not believe these qualities to be energy as we know it. However, given that time and space manifested concurrently with the Big Bang and that the three spatial dimensions are inextricably linked with time, then it would be reasonable to conclude that these four dimensions are a prerequisite for the play and interplay of energy within the physical universe.

Time and spirals

G: Does this relate to the way in which time is moving in our age? I've read in the transcripts of your teachings that time speeds up towards the end of an age, that it has already speeded up and when we move into the Aquarian Age, things will start to slow down again. Now is that somehow linked with the vision that people have at the moment? Is it that anticipation of the Aquarian Age that is causing time to speed up?

M: Not quite. What we are going to say now may seem as though we are going back in reverse to what we have told you, and you will need to think about it. The whole of existence is a spiral. Universal existence is within this ever-moving spiral. It is a spiral of all the energies comprising every molecule, every proton, neutron, everything that is known to science. Its structure is a spiral, and manifests as millions of smaller spirals, but they are all linked to the one spiral that takes in the whole of existence. As it moves inexorably from the beginning, from that first moment, until it ends, (some hundreds and thousands of years hence, in all probability) it takes in all these parent spirals as they manifest and as they share in the progress of what is taking place in the universe. There is a spiral for the Earth, a spiral for each planet, a spiral for the parallel universes, and everything that relates to them.

All these spirals are manifesting in time. Time and space being one energy, they move in accordance with each other, with perfect coordination. The point of the spiral, the smallest part, is always at the end of something that is about to begin again. As it begins to turn again, you see it widening, you see the point of the spirals extending as they turn and they are moving into newness, into that which is to be achieved, is to be experienced by everything that has intelligence. It cannot be experienced by anything inanimate. Therefore, a stone remains as a stone. It cannot change, other than by the dust of ages adhering to it and making it a larger stone. It cannot, for example, turn into a crystal. A drop of water can, because water is a living energy. Are we clear so far?

G: *Yes, Master.*

M: As this spiral continues, and as intelligence links with it, and the vision, as well as the scientific progress takes place, so we move into the new generations, the new aeons of time, the new ages. They have meaning for man because of what has been, what man's memory accepts as truth. Man believes that what has been in the past must continue into the future. It is his dreams that might very well enlarge upon it, and give a more beautiful experience that, as he dreams this, or imagines this, takes place – because everything that takes place in the mind must be experienced in reality. However wild an imagining, or a dream, may appear at the time, it is fixing it within the future as a point to be reached, to be actually experienced. It may not be in that body but maybe as another aspect of the soul which is also moving along the spiral, approaches it and then reaches it. That which we dream of attaining, as the Higher Self absorbs this, and accepts it as its reality, so another aspect of soul will come to Earth, one that is further toward that reality.

Added to this, as the larger, the all-encompassing spiral is spinning, it moves into an age. The age recedes and another age begins to manifest. There comes a point where everything that has occurred in the past meets itself returning. But it meets itself in a higher understanding of intelligence and being. All the progress that has taken place is encapsulated so that when the old awareness meets the new, there is a greater energy that forms, joins, separates, and goes on its way enforced with a greater awareness through the mind, through the molecules within the brain. So that which is achieved as you progress is that much more stable, and in this way you get the purity of physics and mathematics.

You actually see what you have calculated taking place within your life, within the structure that you have built for it, but you do not always know how it is achieved. You do not know how that calculation is actually arrived at, because of what is going on behind the scenes, because of the God force, the God mind that is allowing all of this to take place in such a completely organized and structured manner.

Man's free will has nothing to do with what is actually

achieved. It is outside of his free will. He can come and go, relapse, make his decisions, they are all little puny things to make his life more worthwhile. He always comes back to the fact, to that point that he must arrive at, at a certain moment of achievement. As he arrives at this, so he coordinates with God's vision, God's knowledge of the point at which something will be realized, will be accepted within His scheme of things.

Order and chaos

G: So is the point of achievement something like orderliness that has just come from chaos? Is that the way in which the free will operates? Does it create a variability of patterning, but at some point determined by this point of arrival, this point of attainment, it must all swing in and once again get in step with the motion of the grander scheme of things? Is this the way it works?

M: Yes, it must do this. If it did not then God's existence, that which God is there for, would no longer be, and everything would crash in upon itself. The chaos would return and existence would cease to be.

Entropy

G: There is an analogy for this in the physical world. For instance, you build a house or temple and then over a period of time the building decays. So it is almost as if there is a given point of orderliness and then gradually, over a period of time, the physical structure of the building will inevitably decay unless at a timely point somebody restores that orderliness.

M: It makes a good analogy, we agree, but immediately, of course, we begin to think of matter, and the fact that God's world is in the etheric sense. It cannot destroy, nor be destroyed, nor disintegrate because it does not exist as an object of matter in time – because there is no time. All things that exist within the pattern of time are an illusion.

G: So the analogy would not be in the structure and integrity of the building. Would the orderliness, in fact, be in its design, in its concept, rather than its physical appearance?

M: That is closer. It is the vision of the architect, what he wishes to achieve. And having designed the building and seen it built, he is then satisfied and seldom repeats it. He goes on to improve the design, something better to be achieved on the next occasion.

The significance of water

G: Taking one of the points that you have just raised, you say that water is a living energy. Does that fact explain why something like homeopathy works? In homeopathy it is the dilution of the material in water that gives it its power, which seems quite contrary to the way in which we look at things in the material world, where the expectation is that concentration creates more power.

M: It has a great deal to do with it. There is also the energy of water imbibed into the system that allows the living person to exist. Remove water, remove it from the tissues, remove it from being taken into the body, remove it from the atmosphere that surrounds that body, and it ceases to exist. It is a very, very important energy force for life. All living things need water. Deprive nature of water and it becomes a grain of sand.

G: So water is something like an essence of God?

M: God is indeed within water, the same as God is within everything that lives, whether it is propagated and created by man or whether it is part of the initial creation by God in order that the world might exist and have a reason for existence.

In the mind of God, all things must have a reason for being there; otherwise they do not exist. Everything has its purpose; everything lives on everything else. All things have a complete reason for their existence. When that reason is eliminated, perhaps because they have moved into a time when their existence upon the Earth is no longer feasible, they then are removed to a parallel existence, because there is no death. Nothing can die. Nothing can be eradicated totally; it is either transposed into another form of energy, or it is removed to a different existence where it continues to evolve, to mature, like the dinosaurs.

Planes or spheres of existence and parallel universes

G: So the spheres of existence around the Earth, are they in effect parallel universes?

M: That is correct. The spheres of light where the souls exist are all part of this. They have a different structure, of course.

Spiritual evolution and light bodies

G: *Last time we spoke, we discussed black holes, and we got to the point that at the centre of a black hole would be where God is, in terms of its creative energy and manifestation of the universe. From your previous teachings I understand that when a soul has evolved to the point where no further earthly incarnations are needed, it may ascend to the causal plane, if it has attained the level of knowledge which permits it to become a Master. Beyond that plane of existence, there is a further progression until eventually, as I understand it, you merge with the God force.*

Now, from our discussion about vibration and the nature of a black hole, the idea that I had was that at the centre of a black hole, anything physical could not survive. So is the process of spiritual evolution toward that God force a progressive refining of your light body until such time as it would not be trapped in the black hole and cease to exist?

M: That would be a good explanation.

G: *So what is happening, effectively, is that you are refining your state of being so that it becomes finer and finer, until it reaches the finest, most rarefied, point where you become free from the crushing influence of the enormous force that lies at the centre of the black hole. Presumably, you can then move in and out of the black hole at will. Is that a reasonable proposition?*

M: It is an interesting thought, of moving in and out of the God force at will. It could be possible, but in actual fact it would not occur because, by the time you reach that sense of unity, the desire to be detached would be completely lost. It is almost like a magnet with all things moving toward it with a great desire to be part of it. To be detached, to move away from that source, would be abhorrent. There would also be no motivation, nowhere further that could be attained. It would be a backward step, and the soul desires only progression, to move toward that light, that all-encompassing life force. To move away from it again would not even be considered. But in theory it could be so.

The three aspects of God

The Master teaches that the Christos is one of the three aspects of God. There is the creative, intelligent aspect; the love aspect which is known as the Christos; and the personality aspect which was the incarnated man, Jesus or Yeshua, as He was known, who thus physically embodied the loving personal aspect of God.

Yeshua the personality and the Christos energy

G: I was thinking of this particularly in the light of something like the reawakening, or the re-emergence of the Christos energy. I am presuming that Yeshua went on to merge with the God force and is now shining His light back to the Earth.

M: You are confusing Yeshua the man with the Christos. The Christos was bestowed upon Him, it was not He. He was a manifestation of humanity coming through the same evolutionary scale as any other human being. He was conceived, born, grew from childhood to maturity, and it was at a point of His knowledge, of His acceptance of His path, that the Christos, the all-intelligent manifestation of energy within the centre of God, was bestowed upon Him. It was bestowed upon Him to give Him greater ability, to bring a knowledge that was more than was just inside His consciousness, inside His Higher Self, or His deeper awareness in His soul. It was all-knowing, a total acceptance of reality that He was then able to shine forth to all those that approached Him, those He wished to heal, to teach. It shone forth like a light – that is why He is so often depicted in history with a halo. All humanity has a halo, it is indeed their soul bodies that are surrounding them, but few are seen in the same way as one such as Yeshua had, whose entire physical being was imbued with the radiance of that light.

When He died, then that Christos removed from Him and returned to the source. The very aware and enlightened being that Yeshua, the man, had become moved into a high sphere of light, where, with other manifest beings of light, (the Ascended Masters), He could then bring forth His teaching, His ability to enlighten man through the words and speech and higher intelligence of mankind. He is, of course, in a higher sphere than the causal plane, because of His very ability, His nature, but like all the ascended beings He can travel through those spheres of light and reach others who have not yet reached that Utopia, who are still struggling, still learning, still incarnating, and endeavouring to learn. But it is Yeshua, the man, who is seen in holy places, who is felt by those who reach out to Him. It is the Christos, the knowledge of God, the being of God, that has returned to the source, which now has a much greater energy with it than without it.

We have so enjoyed our conversation, my son, but now we must say farewell. Shalom.

G: Farewell, Master. Shalom.

Chapter 5

Conversation Four

Perception and mind. Absolute truth. Spiritual evolution. The nature of the past, present and future. Mind and its creative power. Spheres of light. Parallel universes and the speed of light. Mediumship. Light streams.

M: Welcome, my son. Shalom.

G: *Welcome, Master. Shalom.*

M: It has been quite a little while since we spoke in this manner but, as always, it delights us to be able to speak upon those matters that give us such pleasure.

Perception and mind

G: *The last time we spoke we were talking about time and space. I'm still not totally clear about these concepts. My understanding of time and space now is that we experience a virtual reality whereby everything that happens around us is a projection into this space. I rather view it like being in a cinema where there is a screen, which is in itself unchanging. Projected upon that screen is a film and it is that unchanging screen which is the basis of time and space and the film is like the world that we actually experience. The awareness of that screen is the perception of a soul in a higher state of awareness. Would this be an accurate description?*

M: As far as that goes, yes. But there is also the concept of mind to be brought into this picture. The reality of what is taking place must also have its own perception. It must be translated into a phenomenon that can be both acceptable and also duplicated for not just one, but many. The aspect can be a little different according to those that are viewing it, their position, their concept, their reality, as it might be called.

If in the middle of this screen it was conceived that a flower would be apparent, whoever it is that is visualizing the flower could well put one of hundreds of different varieties within that space, from memory, from what the mind has conceived. But if there is the original to be perceived, if there is one flower that must be synchro-imposed upon that screen, it still depends upon the viewpoint of those that are looking upon it. Whether they are looking from above or below. Whether they are looking at it within the daylight or at night and so on. So you then get many different perceptions of that one flower which is being perceived by mankind. The mind plays a very important part in what is remembered or what is visualized as another describes it. This brings about so many different perceptions that to say of any one item that it is the absolute truth, the total reality, is impossible. For example, with the many colours that exist, two people may not visualize exactly the same shade as each other. Does this throw any more light upon it?

Absolute truth
I have – in common with many, I suspect – always thought that truth would be an absolute indisputable quality recognized by all, regardless of age, culture or intellect, a single unified body of knowledge which encapsulates the whole experience of life. But it seems that there is more to it than that, that truth is not static!

G: I had thought that mind would actually come into the picture and I did wonder whether it was the mind of God or the mind of man that created the projection. If we go into the park and there is an oak tree growing in the park, do we not all see the same tree? Presumably we, as a collective mind, have created this tree growing there. It would seem inconceivable to me that if I decide that the tree is going to be an oak and somebody else decides it is going to be a beech that the tree would manifest differently to each of us.

M: That was not what we meant. We agree that both people would perceive the oak – but different aspects of the oak. Some might concentrate on a section of the bark while another might concentrate upon the boughs or the leaves and the shape of the leaf. Different people's perceptions of size vary considerably. So you cannot really assume that the perception of the depth of colour, or the number of leaves, would be the same to both of the viewers. If both had a talent for drawing or sketching and were asked to sit in similar positions and to sketch that tree you would then see the perception of one next to the other and how accurate they both are as to what is actually there before them. The mind plays an important part in all memory because a childhood scene remembered by one would have a different aspect to that remembered by another. A child's memory is weaker than that of an adult, for example.

G: *So we are talking here about an object creating an impression in the mind of an observer and that the differences lie in the way in which the observer perceives the tree through the senses and through their assessment of things like shape, colour, size. So that two artists painting the same tree would produce very different interpretations because it has gone through their subjective mind.*

M: Exactly. If two artists were drawing or painting a general scene, that of cottages with their gardens and trees surrounding them, then one object would be more to the forefront than another, according to that artist's perception.

Spiritual evolution

I was still trying to determine and understand exactly what changes as a soul evolves and how this change manifests and affects the life of an incarnated aspect.

G: *As I understand the spiritual evolution of mankind, the perceptions of an individual as they evolve spiritually become more refined. Is the process of refining becoming more aware of the screen rather than the projection upon it? Is that the process in terms of the mind of a person who is evolving spiritually?*

M: It is rather more the perception of what is upon the screen than the screen itself – which you may have meant, of course. But there again, as each person develops in a different way in their spiritual awakening and gifts, so different things would be created very differently one from another. The facets of knowledge, which arises from deep within the soul of an individual's spiritual understanding, can be many and varied, almost as the grains of sand upon the shore. Your concept of God and what has been created within the universe specifically by the idea of God might be very different from that which a more prosaic, possibly scientifically orientated person would perceive. Each one adopts a different attitude of mind, considering their concept of life and reality as opposed to another person's concept of a similar viewpoint upon that screen. What you find important, another may disregard.

It is like the artist looking at the scenery. He may totally disregard the cottages as being unimportant to nature and the cottages may not even exist within the painting or be relegated to the background as he concentrates upon the design and colour of nature. He may even be more aware of the sunshine as it highlights the different aspects of his drawing, while another would disregard this and find part of the cottage grasps his view to the exclusion of all else. This is what makes the mind of man so infinitely individual to the personality. The mind of God has its own definite perception from which the reality of creation was fashioned. But mankind's awareness of creation and what is important within it may differ considerably. The brain enables man to discuss his perceptions. This is very important because, through discussion with others, he is enabled to create an individual point of view. If the discussion did not exist, then those who have a narrower view of life would find it very difficult to broaden their view and open up to new possibilities.

G: I have a concept which takes the idea of watching a projection on a screen a little further. If we imagine for one moment that we are sitting in a cinema and we are watching a film. Now, one can enter into the illusion of what is happening in front of one and actually be there and feel all the intensity of the emotion and action of everything that is going on. But there is a point in life, and you may be able to do this through meditation, where you can draw your perception back and become aware of yourself sitting in your seat in the cinema and watching this happen without actually being involved with it. Now is that the state of experiencing absolute truth – the awareness of the cinema rather than just being aware of the screen?

The power of the mind and free will
M: We would agree with this perception of absolute truth. However, because man has been given a series of gifts and choices, among which is the ability to draw upon memory which colours his perception of what is taking place, it does overshadow his own ability to stand back and be aware without being actively involved. As the eyes rove, so also do the concentration and the ability of the mind to focus itself clearly on its objective.

Other creatures in creation are better able to have a complete perception, because they have limited ability to remember the past, or to project their minds forward into the future, on the basis of what has gone before. It is only mankind that has that ability. The animal world is conscious of what is taking place around it at any given time. Fear can be involved in certain actions or certain realities which enable that animal in the future to avoid certain scenarios or events, but it does not reason why. Any event, whether it is enacted by the person or animal who originally created that fear or by another, creates exactly the same emotion.

However, where man is concerned, his imagination of an event can be as real while it is taking place as when the memory brings it back before the gaze. So it is the same with this cinema screen. As different enactments take place, the concept of the story within the imagination brings about certain reactions. This can colour the experience of an event, predisposing one to predict a particular finale. What occurs then is that the ability of man to create for himself, to make his own decisions, to alter events through his concepts, brings about a different expectation from that which the director originally conceived, causing surprise if that finale is different.

In a more practical sense, the world as it now is has been changed by the vision of man, not by the vision of God. God's vision, God's creation could remain virtually at a standstill if it were not for man's ability to bring about changes through action and interaction. The only change that God might bring about would be as a natural result of all the essence that He has created, which would bring about a gentler flow and a more positive reaction with less destruction – if any at all, because God's concept is of that which is everlasting and not destructive. Does this make sense to you?

Parallel lives

G: Yes. I think the source of my puzzlement about time and space is something we mentioned when we were speaking about this before: that everything that was, is and will be, exists concurrently at this present time. It leads me to think that rather than just looking at a screen where the events of the present are being projected and are obviously flowing forward into the future, we could be said to be looking at an infinite number of screens on which everything is being projected simultaneously. So that, if everything that was still exists and everything that will be already exists then does that mean, for instance, that those incarnations are still taking place now? As I live in this life, are other aspects of my Higher Self which were living 200, 400, 1,000 years ago still present there and living their lives?

M: That is so, because there are so many planes of existence where the activities of different ages continue to evolve and to come to their fulfilment. All these different parallel existences have come about as a result of different concepts, effecting a radical change due to certain events that have taken place. So all these different directions are very like a series of roads that lead to the same destination. You choose the road which gives the view that you wish to enjoy upon that route, upon that travelling toward the destination. It is, of course, far more vast than this, but all explanations must be of a very simple nature in order to create an understanding of that which is more complex.

The nature of the past, present and future
I now see time in a very much more expanded way and find it helps to think of all the incarnating aspects (i.e. every incarnation you have ever experienced; see page 86 and also Appendix I under Higher Self) living concurrently, rather like characters in their own television dramas, each one on a different channel spaced out along the frequency range. By tuning to a particular frequency it becomes possible to view one programme and then, by retuning the receiver to a new frequency, to see a quite different play on a different channel. The signal for all channels is present but it is only the tuning frequency that determines the channel and play that you watch.

If you can imagine your world, with what is taking place within it at this time and then consider that every change of direction or event has the potential to produce a different end product, then you have the possibility of infinite worlds being created. We have already spoken of the fact that the world of the dinosaurs still exists and that those creatures are still living within it. And yet certain events which occurred within your world finalized the existence of the dinosaurs and other vast creatures and propelled them, as it were, into a parallel world.

You can see how difficult it is to have one specific conception of any event because the mind is continually creating. As something which you have visualized and conceived takes place, you might imagine a different outcome. That outcome is then manifest somewhere within the infinite space that is the universe and the many other universes. These other universes cannot be perceived by man because they are of a different vibrational speed [frequency].

Mind and its creative power
It is often said in esoteric teachings that the mind is very powerful and can create our reality. Just how powerful it is, and the mechanism by which this works, is perhaps not understood or experienced by us as a concrete reality.

Mind and creation
Man doesn't always realize that his visualization of different events can actually create the reality of it, but it is indeed so. So that which was the blueprint for creation from the mind of God has all these concepts and abilities to engender change. What you are describing is like a camera shutting down after each still frame has been taken, as opposed to the flowing narrative of a cinema film.

The mind can do this. It is infinite, it is not simply confined to the individual personality, it can reach out. The spirit world is part of this. At the end of the existence of the individual, when he can no longer exist in his world of matter, because different factors exist to prevent the continuity, he continues his life in another world with different values and in a body which is an exact replica of the one that he has just shed. The etheric body still continues its existence, content to fulfil that which the soul aspect has visualized.

As we teach, the complexity of the soul has all the aspects of the Higher Self animated into a separate existence. How can each aspect of the soul possibly continue its progression, if it were to have continuous lives, one after another, in the same world and with the same cinematic screen before it? It could not do so. So it moves in and out of all these different concepts as it desires to fulfil certain growth, be it spiritual growth or the growth of the personality only.

Spheres of light
Most of us imagine that the spirit world, if we accept such a concept, is somewhere 'out there' in the vastness of space, that heaven is somewhere in the sky, beyond the clouds. But with the mystery of space now being probed by our satellites, it is difficult to retain that picture in the light of scientific knowledge today.

The vibrational model of creation allows a more coherent picture of the spiritual domain and our physical world to coexist, each in its own reality on its own frequency beyond the bounds of the physical universe, beyond time and space and yet overlaying our experience of reality. After all, even this rock-solid physical universe is 99% empty space. (In the simple model of the atom, the building block of physics, there is a small nucleus with a number of orbiting electrons, the remainder being a void.)

G: *Following on from this particular discussion, I have a few questions relating to the spheres of light and I think we have touched upon these. Do all the spheres of light exist in the same space just separated by a vibrational frequency?*

M: Everything in existence, whatever it may be within the universe, actually is in the same space, but at a different vibration. Some vibrations can be seen, such as the planetary outline – now, of course, much closer with the instruments that man has created for himself. But there are other existences, other universes, which man cannot perceive, even though they are there before him, because the vibrational rate is not one which is within his perception.

We think you have put this very lucidly and in a way that most people could accept when reading such a theory.

Parallel universes and the speed of light
Our own universe seems to have a governing universal speed which appears to be determined by the speed of light. I wondered if there are multiples of the speed of light with a different universe within each multiple?

G: *Is the process of moving toward the truth, in terms of its absolute form, really refining your ability to perceive in terms of the different frequencies and speeds of light? So that, in fact, you then have access to the fuller range of parallel universes? Because if you can perceive four times the speed of light you may get four different separate universes which you can see in multiples of the speed of light. For instance, the physical world that we inhabit exists from zero up to the speed of light. We then go through the barrier at the speed of light to a different reality which would be between the speed of light and twice the speed of light, and simi-*

larly from two to three and three to four times the speed of light. In this way it would be possible to perceive the parallel universes which make up the spiritual spheres. Is that the way that one's perception and awareness naturally grow?

Acceptance

M: It does; but, of course, the perception takes many hundreds and thousands of years and different lifetimes to be able to accept the principle of what you are saying before the actual energies which are used for this perception can indeed be utilized. Ancient man – shall we say, the very first being to stand upright, to separate himself from the animal world – could not possibly conceive within his brain or his ability of mind what you are now able to give voice to, that you can now perceive as a possibility becoming a reality. Maybe in many lifetimes to come you would then devise a way in which that conception could become a reality, enabling you to separate the particles within your sight so that you could see these different realities and different worlds in a logical and harmonious way.

Many scientists can now conceive a reality from which they are able to present their blueprint, but they do not yet have the ability to allow it to become manifest within the reality of their experiments. Man is working toward this slowly, tenuously, but it is occurring. Primitive man would not even conceive of what would lie behind the clouds; present-day man can not only use instruments which show him what lies beyond them, but can actually travel there himself in many instances. Where he is too frail to allow his own body to travel, he can create instruments which will do it on his behalf. But look how long it has taken for these two events to take place. If you extrapolate from this, it will be many hundreds and thousands of years, if not a million years, before man can actually perceive through his instruments a different universe.

Humanity currently has a concept of time and space which does not coordinate with the reality of time and space being instant and being part of the same creative ability as that of the God force. It is impossible still for the majority of mankind to conceive a God that is pure energy. If this cannot be conceived, despite all the efforts of science and scientists, then how can he even conceive the possibility of parallel worlds and passing from one to another by allowing his own body to manifest and de-manifest within its particles to allow this to take place?

What at the moment is pure science fiction will eventually become reality when man accepts it as a concept that can occur – and when he accepts this, it will occur. How else do you think it is possible for the spirit beings who lived thousands of years ago to be able to enter into the body, as it were, as in mediumship, of those living upon the Earth at this time and to speak their truth, their knowledge through humanity? It is through a transposition of those very particles that have been created throughout time in order to relate to those that have incarnated at this particular time and who have speech and movement.

How the Master manifests

G: So does the way in which this works mean that you and the channel through whom you speak occupy the same space at the present time and that you can both be aware of one another when this happens?

M: That is correct. We have described it in the past as the ability of her soul complex to gradually grow with knowledge so that it reaches out through the planes of light while our understanding and reality reaches towards her soul. It then blends with it and travels down like a pathway of light, taking but a split second to reach her mind. So it becomes unified, it becomes one thought, one action, one ability to give voice. It is not something that simply occurs at will. It has to gradually develop, with the soul's cooperation, throughout the months and years, until eventually this interaction can take place.

There are many who would sit where you now are, and because of their ability for psychic sight would not see our channel but would see Joseph where she sits. It would be very difficult for that person to be able to describe satisfactorily to another how they perceive and where it is that the human form has gone to enable the etheric of another once-human form to take its place. It can only be achieved through the acceptance of the principle of parallel lives and the fact that what occurred 2,000 years ago is still taking place and also able to merge with what is taking place within the world at this moment. If that is accepted as a possibility and it is harmonized by a person who has the beginnings of this form of sight, then you can see that at some time it will be possible to perceive the other universes as well as those that exist within them, and the parallel lives that they are enjoying at this very moment.

When the future for man is being discussed, there is this basic inability to move away from the screen image that he is now looking at in order to perceive what is not yet reality, or even could be a reality in future. Certainly man two or three billion years ago, in the way that he perceived the world, would not even visualize his own progress the way that man can now with the abilities that he has developed. In the same way, a simple animal would not be able to visualize being a human being, even though he dwells with one and is able to relate to the thoughts going through man's mind, intercepting them, interpreting them without need of words, simply by utilizing its own basic instincts. Yet that thought takes form and is accepted without the need of language, without even the need of words. The animal and the human relate together in that one space.

G: So the means by which you come here today and speak with me is really by a meeting of soul and mind between yourself and your channel which enables you to bridge the gap between the causal plane and the earthly plane?

M: There is no gap. The causal plane and the Earth plane are united together except for that vibration which apparently separates them because of the lack of perception through the human eye and through the human brain – not mind, brain.

Move away from the eye, move away from the brain, sit where you are with eyes closed, trying not to perceive a reality through logic. Just accept that the soul of Joseph and the soul of our channel are at this moment united, allowing the ability of speech to take place. The only difficulty is through words, through the acceptance of language and words being different between the reality of Joseph and the reality of our channel. Accept those concepts and you have bridged the etheric world and the human world and allowed them to merge together. Then you accept their merging together, without any logic of space intervening, without considering that the etheric world is somewhere in space that cannot be perceived. It is in reality occupying the same space as is occupied by the world itself. The only difference is the vibration and the light which separates us from the reality of your sight and your brain.

G: As I closed my eyes and tried to experience this I found a very powerful feeling of expansion, as if I had broken the boundaries of my physical body. There was a sense of lightness and a colour, which I can only describe as deep purple.

M: You entered into the reality of the true analysis of existence which is colour. Everything is vibration within colour. It is from the colour spectrum that everything emerged and is, of course, broken down in the particles of light within your flower, within your tree. When it returns to the light particles from which it is comprised you see then only the colour spectrum which is in actuality the tree and the flower.

So, as you endeavoured, without the illusion of sight, to visualize the two souls together you saw the colour shared between the two souls, which was the deep purple – which has, we understand, been shown in great clarity through the medium of a camera fairly recently, although the visual representation of the human being was also present in the Kirlian photograph [a form of photography which claims to capture on film the human aura]. The colour predominates and the colour is the deciding factor of unity within the two souls. If there had been a different colour spectrum between them, the unity would not be possible in the same way – which, of course, leads us to why it is that there are some that can channel and some that cannot. If they do not reach the colour vibration with those whom they wish to channel – or those who wish to channel through them, which is more accurate – then it cannot be achieved. This is more fully explained in our teaching on light streams.

Light streams
This concept is explained more fully in a sister publication entitled The Way of Soul where you will find a description of the meaning of the colours of the light streams which denote the soul's path of learning. (See also page 151 in Appendix I, on Light streams.)

M: How is our time with you?

G: *Unfortunately, we have run out of time, Master.*

M: It passes so quickly my son, does it not? Until next time, farewell. Shalom.

Chapter 6

Conversation Five

Thought, mind and emotion. Intuition. The purpose of life. Extinction. Global warming. Aspects of the Higher Self and the spiritual spheres. The Children of Light.

M: Welcome, my son. Shalom.

G: *Welcome, Master. Shalom.*

The nature of thought
Gradually, through our discussions, I had become more aware of the power of the mind and that the medium through which the mind communicates involves thoughts and feelings. I was now particularly interested to find out whether all thoughts exist in a pool at which all can drink or whether there is a more personal aspect to thinking.

G: *As I understand it, creation really is a thought in the mind of God and the thought is energy.*

M: Indeed.

G: *Is the mind a receptacle of thought or does it tap into some other vast area of energy and then create thoughts from it?*

M: A little of both. Take for example the animal world, especially the more advanced animals, the monkey family, the dolphins, which always create so much thought within humanity as to whether they have ever been human. We have spoken quite often about dolphins to individuals. Now, they have a collective mind. Many talk of the collective soul but they don't really understand the connotations here. The mind is also collective and the way in which these animals work is that they pick up what is understood about life from all their species. So they are able to contact each other without language. They have a certain amount of language when they are together, of course they do, but they do not express it through words in the same way that humankind can do. So it is important that through their mind they are able to contact each other and to know what is taking place amongst their own species.

There is also a greater mind which combines all the species of animals together. So, let us say, the cat can relate to the mouse, understand exactly what the mouse is about and its function. Then the insect world is also able to relate together; an ant colony, a bee colony, they all interrelate through thought. So the collective mind is very important for the animal world. To a lesser extent the same is true in the world of nature, trees interrelate, plants, shrubs ... So there is that which is for the species and that which is for the general awareness of all of nature itself.

It is more refined in human beings. Thought can be expressed verbally because human beings have a closer relationship to that aspect of the God force than does nature and the animal world. This is not understood in general, either scientifically or philosophically. These aspects are supposed to exist only in the realm of fantasy and therefore beyond the general questioning power of mankind. So we feel it is quite important that this book presents a picture that people can learn from, so that they understand some of the particular concepts rather more than they would without this knowledge.

G: So is the mind of man more refined because it is closer to the God force?

Crystal mind
M: 'Refined' perhaps would not be the way we would seek to describe it. In fact, it is difficult to find a word ... It is more advanced. It has more ability to reason. Animals don't reason. Animals work with their senses so their contact with the God force is through sense and not through decision-making, not through free will which, of course, man has domination of. There are really three categories of existence that we relate to specifically: man, animal, and mineral.

So there is even a conscious mind relating to minerals such as crystals, and crystals do communicate. They have to communicate, otherwise how would different crystals harmonize together for their healing tasks? If they do not communicate on some level of understanding, they would conflict. But again, there is the communal mind of, say, an amethyst and a more collective knowledge or consciousness of all the crystals within the knowledge of the universe.

The result of man's thought and emotion
G: So when we look at man and the soul aspect within man, am I correct in thinking that the love aspect, and the free will aspect actually create something, perhaps as a result of man experiencing the love aspect?

M: There are certain emotional results of the ability of man to think which actually exude from his physical body and help other species to relate to him, as well as the relationships between man himself. Mostly it is through smell but there is also a relationship created through the ability of the body to exude through its cellular structure other, more subtle, methods of communication. These are acceptable to all species because there are those species that do not smell. If there were not something which warned each species of the approach of other species they would have no chance whatsoever of survival.

It is very much like man's emotional relationship to the energies of the Moon. Some have a very intense emotional reaction which shows in many different ways. No one would argue the fact that the link between man's emotions and this particular planetary force is very strong indeed, and all the different planets have their own characteristic mode of communication. It is not done through man's senses; it is through his emotional body, which picks up the radar signal you might say, and interprets it according to the ability of those planets to form their own kind of communication. It is all very finely done, very subtly done.

G: Yes, I see.

Communication with the God force
M: But it is done constantly and not just upon certain occasions or when it is needed to be finely tuned; it is indeed always there. Man does his formal tuning and fine-tuning as and when he feels related to the source. Man communicates with the God energy in the same way. Man does it consciously by relating to the God force either with a prayer or with a request, whereas animals have a different way of relating because they cannot consciously think and make choices.

Man once had the same kind of knowledge as animals, before he became conversant with language. But he has largely lost his ability to hear and to smell and also to be guided by instinct. This is because he relies on other forces to guide him, through his mind, his more intellectual abilities.

Intuition

G: *Yes, it does seem that man has moved towards the intellectual, particularly in the way that he uses his brain. What part does intuition play in the mind of man?*

M: Through the ancient mystics of the very early incarnations of man, when he was still relating to a great extent to the animal world – going back, of course, to the time when he was barely upright in his abilities – the instinct that you might have as to whether somebody is speaking the truth or whether they are a loyal friend, this comes from these ancient abilities and which linger within your Higher Self, which also in part relates to those particular times.

G: *I see the intuition, from my perspective, as something that is higher than the intellect. It's almost like a higher faculty of the mind. Would that be a correct statement?*

M: Indeed so, because it is formed by very refined energies, whereas the intellect is gained by the momentum of acquiring knowledge through scholastic ability. You are quite right when you say that the brain is now more active and has greater knowledge. Anything that comes down through the ages, improving all the time with the knowledge that is gained from mobility, from travel, from association with other races, must, of course, expand within its knowledge. Whereas in the days when mankind lived on his own little island, and even broken down within different forestry groups within that island, never meeting each other, then there was a different process of learning and of being aware of one another. Everything must expand and grow; that is the purpose of creation. The fact that it takes so long is because of man's inability to relate to anything that is not proven.

The purpose of life

G: *So what is the purpose of life? Taking the fact that we incarnate here to connect with our soul purpose, what is the criterion by which a life is judged successful?*

M: The ultimate aim of all humanity is a closeness with the intelligence, the knowledge of the God force. With each incarnation that is lived – certainly with each spiritual incarnation – there is a greater ability to rise above what is taking place on the Earth and move into the spectrum of the God force, to have the ability to enter, to link into that energy, to accept that energy as a living vibration of life. When that occurs, then that energy will be greatly expanded upon and life as it is now formed will cease to be. It will not be relevant to what is needed for the understanding of soul. Man's body, his relationship to matter, is only in order that he may, step by step, move into the intellectual boundaries of that energizing God force, with the acceptance of total reason, total understanding of how creation came to be.

Man is a long way from forming this ultimate knowledge, a very long way. We can project at least two ages ahead [an astrological age lasts approximately two thousand years] before man begins to link his mind directly with the God force with understanding. Each stage he reaches, he thinks he has an absolute knowledge but when he has that absolute knowledge he will not need to think he has it; it will be a knowing, it will be a part of what he is at that stage. It will be the gradual loosening of the need for the body, with all its parts, and the merging, first into the etheric, which is the first stage of that acceptance. In each sphere through which man progresses he loses more and more of the ability to be 'I' and merges with the 'I am', with the totality of life, until at the highest stage that man can become, which is in the causal, he still has the ability to be individual. After that, that ability is gone and the remaining stages involve moving closer and closer to the Absolute until complete absorption. When it happens, the world will be relegated to a planetary energy which will relate to the other planets and will not relate to man's desire for progression.

Extinction

The reason why much of the animal world is becoming extinct is not as scientists believe: that modern living, pollution and the use of insecticides and other such pollutionary objects are causing the extinction of species. It is because those species are no longer required upon the Earth. Can you imagine a dinosaur being needed? That great huge clumsy creature with the smallest pea of a brain, being needed in the 21st century? There are other species, many of them of the insect life, that scientists are desperately trying to preserve. They are only doing this so that they may acknowledge that the species existed and to do tests upon it as to what its function really is and whether it is essential for present-day living.

Endangered species become so because the species as a whole gradually loses its ability to reproduce. This is happening, of course, now with the pandas and the desperate efforts of zoologists to preserve the species will be to no avail. Within the next century they will disappear as will many others, the lions and the tigers, some of the monkey family and a great deal of mammals. But those mammals that do have something greater than instinct, such as the dolphins who have been around in a form of their species since Atlantis, will survive. Although at that time they were not dolphins; they were another species bordering on the dolphin, even more highly intellectual than they are now. They were never humankind, any more than the half-man, half-animal species that worked with the Atlanteans and the early Egyptians.

G: Many people take the view that the plight of these animals is caused by man. Does this mean that man's activity upon the Earth is not the sole cause of the present extinction that we see?

Man's activity upon the Earth and Global warming
M: It is part of the process of elimination of unnecessary life, unnecessary species.

G: In the present situation that the Earth is in, it strikes me very forcibly that mankind is continually overexploiting the natural resources of the Earth.

M: That is true.

G: And in many areas we are actually deforesting the Earth.

M: Which is to its detriment.

G: Is this a natural process?

M: It is part of a process which is taking place a little too early. The global warming is a necessary consequence of the Sun coming closer to the Earth, but it is happening much too soon because of man's neglect of his stewardship of the Earth. Probably in another 200-300 years through natural processes man would reach what is taking place now with far less ill effect. He finds this process deeply disturbing because physiologically he is not prepared for it and the essence of man, along with animal, mineral and planetary life, all work in a particular spiral which forms the process of evolution. If any of this is hastened it loses its synchronicity and therefore man feels this to be an unnatural process. But if you went back to cavemen and suddenly put them in with the present generation of people, they could not survive it. Nor yet if you put man now back into that time, he could not survive it. This is the reason why evolution takes place so phenomenally slowly.

Man and society

G: So I presume the way that man treats man at the moment is the result of this imbalance because we do have a very exploitative attitude. Those of us in the developed world exploit the less developed world and so on. And even in the developed world the rich exploit the poor, in many respects. What is the ideal society for mankind to actually embark upon?

M: The ideal society is to share equally amongst all the human species. But this has never been so. There have always been the jealousies, the desire to be greater than those who are weaker. All the while there are the stronger and the weaker within the species there will be this lack of ability to accept a weaker force, to accept that which cannot fight for itself in order to survive. The fighting spirit of man is that which needs to give way to the spiritual awareness through that God force which is available to all. But where ignorance reigns, where man is unable to attain this knowledge through his location perhaps, or his inability to relate on an intellectual level, then he will always be the weaker of the species and will be prey to those who have a greater life force and a greater desire to achieve.

In a way, the intellect, when it began to create modes of transport, was meant to alleviate this. It was meant to allow areas of the world that knew less to gain from the greater knowledge of other areas. It has never worked out in that way and now man relies so totally on intellect and so narrowly accepts his spiritual essence that probably it will be another 100 years at least before any parity is attained.

G: One of the ideas which I have had along these lines starts from Darwin and The Origin of the Species, the concept of the survival of the fittest. The idea that life is a struggle, and very often an uneven struggle, for some species and for some aspects of mankind, when taken to its logical extreme would entail a society, which in many respects would almost be anarchic, very like organized crime, a despotic society. My ideas around this were that the thing that prevents this taking place is our connection with our soul element, our compassion and our love, and the conscience, accessed through the Higher Self. That is really the idea that I would wish to convey in this book, that man is more than just an animal struggling for survival upon the planet.

M: Indeed so. [Said with emphasis.]

Aspects of the Higher Self and the spiritual spheres
The Master teaches that around the planet Earth there are a total of twelve spiritual spheres, although he generally acknowledges seven main spheres, referring to the remaining five as 'sub-vales' of spiritual existence, finer distinctions within a particular level of being.

The first three spheres, the etheric, are where the soul resides after death, each graded according to the level of attainment and understanding of the returning aspect of soul. The term aspect refers to the incarnated soul fragment with its personality, which is part of a much larger entity called the Higher Self, or total soul. This total soul is a composite of all aspects that have lived or have a potential to live. The total soul decides when an aspect needs to incarnate upon the Earth for its learning experience and upon death the aspect returns to the spiritual spheres and shares its knowledge with the whole. At this point the Higher Self may then decide that further incarnations are required for its progression. This new aspect has an entirely different personality to any other aspect. It is also possible for many aspects to incarnate at the same time into different circumstances to maximize the learning potential of a particular period of time or set of events.

Beyond the first three spheres lie the astral sphere, or plane, and the causal plane. The astral is where the soul is able to progress its knowledge in the Halls of Learning. We have already spoken of the causal plane, where the Masters of Light reside and teach. It is at this level that Master Joseph himself exists, and he has explained that these two spheres of light are closely linked, since the Masters themselves will continue to learn and teach in the Halls of Learning. Beyond this sphere is the plane of Nirvana where the soul is absorbed into the light and is no longer a separate entity. The seventh sphere is the merging with the God force, the ultimate reality of Truth.

Spiritual evolution

G: It seems to me that we dispense with the body when we move through the seven spirit spheres but, whilst we are on the Earth, we can also access areas of the spirit world through meditation and through our connection with our Higher Self. As humankind evolves further towards the light, does the physics of each of those layers actually change?

M: Ultimately yes it does, because as the soul evolves towards the light it has the effect on the human body of raising certain levels of both expectancy and deep inner knowledge, which must continue to go through the whole process. So as the aspects of the soul absorb what is given to them by the latest incarnating aspect within existence, so all of the soul aspects benefit from the progression.

This leads to the awareness that as each sphere increases its ability to understand and relate to the God force, so ultimately the initial spheres, that of the etheric in its first, second and third levels, evolve to become an integral part of the astral. Then the astral and the causal will become integrated, losing these earlier stages of progression in the spirit body in the soul form. This will continue in this way over the next few thousand years until man becomes far more aware of his spiritual essence and will lose his warring desires and expanding intellectual growth over the needs of the body. But again it is, of course, a slow process and everything must harmonize.

The wild animals that devour each other in order to continue their existence will become extinct and the gentler animals that relate more together, they will predominate. There will be a greater flow of those species until none are needed on the planet and this in itself, as extinction continues to occur, does affect humankind and his ability to survive.

The future of mankind

G: So the aggression which is in the mind of man at the present time actually creates the predatory species existing upon the Earth? It's almost as if the vibrational elements from our mind create the fact that we actually see a nature that is red in tooth and claw.

M: Indeed.

G: That is a very, very profound thought. It is almost, as man is, so nature is.

M: Exactly. We doubt whether you will get purely scientific people to accept this in the present time. But the Children of Light are the hope for mankind, the embodiment of the logic of man's more spiritual nature joining with his intellect.

The Children of Light

These are very special children born at the dawn of the Aquarian Age. They are fully realized beings who have no need to incarnate upon the Earth but have chosen to do so to lead mankind away from the precipice toward which he is heading. This subject is described in detail in a monograph, The Children of Light, devoted entirely to these children, the eldest of whom are now in their early twenties. (See also page 162 in Appendix I.)

There are many who will want to know what will eventually be the end product, you might say, of their existence – because they [the children] are only just coming into their own and none of them have really any kind of status within the world as yet, the eldest is still too young. But of course preparation has been made by many more advanced spiritual people for these Children of Light to be absorbed into their spectrum of understanding and move through that to a greater ability to change the world into something more spiritual.

G: That's a very reassuring picture of the future of mankind.

M: We do hope that it will be acceptable to your readers. Now, we realize that we have only a few minutes left, so we will take this opportunity to say farewell to you, my son. Shalom.

Chapter 7

Conversation Six

Dark matter. Planet Earth. Planetary life and beings. UFOs. Regenerating the body. God and scientists. The Aum and the music of the spheres. The myth of Lucifer.

M: Welcome, my son. Shalom.

G: Welcome, Master. Shalom.

M: We are all mustered ready to give, we hope, concise replies to the questions that you have prepared. So shall we begin?

Dark matter

G: When we look at the universe, we see galaxies revolving around in space and what is understood is that these galaxies actually revolve at a much faster rate than would appear possible if the matter that we see is all that there is. So there is postulated a theory that in fact there is some other binding energy or something that is known as 'dark matter', which holds everything in place. I wonder whether dark matter is something like love or some spiritual energy rather than an actual physical material?

M: That is an interesting theory – not quite the way that we would perhaps have seen it or expressed it because that is not our concept of love. Our concept of love is expression; it is using energy in such a way that it brings about creative impulses, the ability to see what is inspiring and good in what is around man. Whereas the kind of love which is often suggested when speaking of creation and God isn't love at all; it is balance, harmony, the ability of everything within creation to work in such a way that it is limited to its own resources and doesn't interfere with that which emanates from anything else within the universal structure.

This, again, is very difficult to put into clear words for people to be able to see a very lucid picture of what is really taking place in the universe and in all those millions of different structures which are moving around in space and which nonetheless don't collide and don't destroy each other.

So it is rather more a form of magnetism than love. The magnetic field surrounding everything that has been created either draws to it that which will benefit it or it repels that which is harmful. There have only been one or two recorded calamities which have truly affected Earth in a major way, of some of the rocks in space that have bludgeoned into the Earth and which have created such havoc in so doing. But they never knocked the Earth off course, and science doesn't seem to look at that, doesn't think, 'Well, with such an enormous obstacle flying through space, embedding itself within the face of the Earth, how come it didn't knock it off course, move it from its axis?' That is always something that we feel one day some bright spark will say: 'Let's look into this, let's see what stabilizes the Earth truly within its own space so that nothing that happens to it actually destroys it or makes it take a different course.'

Now, of course, we know all the scientific data about how it turns and how every 26,000 or so years there are these little very vital variances which are hardly even worth considering when you think of everything else that is in space. When you think a shooting star is as vast in its size as the whole of Australia, for example, and yet it shoots, and when it comes within a radius of the Earth ... pop! It's disappeared!

So there is a magnetic field which protects the Earth and which prevents anything truly inharmonious happening to it all the while Earth is essential within the configuration of planets.

G: *Well, that's very interesting, Master. Certainly the meteorite impacts that have been discovered do occasionally seem to be rather vast and there are areas of the world where – for example, the whole Caribbean Sea is thought to be a one-time crater of a meteorite impact, which is enormous.*

M: There again, remember our other teaching about things changing but nothing is destroyed. Although the land mass was turned into a crater, that became the receptacle for further oceans, rather than losing other land masses with the encroachment of masses of water flowing over them.

G: *Yes, absolutely.*

M: So who is to say or not to say that that was a preconceived event?

G: *Yes, there is an intelligence in all of this, isn't there?*

M: Oh, absolutely, and intelligence, of course, is a word we would use rather more than love when you are talking about dark matter, antimatter, what is prevailing out there in space. We would say it is intelligence.

G: So in a way planetary forces and planetary beings are created from the first principle, the intelligence aspect of God, whilst soul is created really by the love aspect, the Christos?

M: Yes. Well, soul was always there but it turned to the love aspect to give it free will.

Planet Earth
G: I've been looking into the nature of the universe as we see it, as we experience it in our physical plane. I look out into the night sky and I read scientific journals that explain to me that there is a lot of orderliness in the universe itself. Yet within physics there is something called the Second Law of Thermodynamics, which actually says that there is a natural tendency for all systems in the physical universe to tend toward decay unless some energy, some work or maintenance is expended upon them. For example, a building will eventually collapse if it is not maintained properly; a garden, if not properly tended, will become overgrown and chaotic. Now it seems to me that what we have here is a universe which is contrary to what we would expect from the Second Law of Thermodynamics, contrary to the nature of the physical universe. I'm wondering if that orderliness has really been implanted there by the intelligent nature of the creative principles of the God force.

M: Let us look at the Earth itself for a moment. You have noted correctly that the chaotic principle, if we may call it that, reigns supreme in every part of the Earth, whether it is due to decay, whether it is due to too frequent additions of everything – the way it multiplies and grows – until it engenders its own ability, not simply to propagate itself but also to destroy itself through too great numbers, rather like humankind is doing at the moment. If it continues to multiply in the present way there will be insufficient food, habitation or land for man to live upon. Now, the reason that the Earth works under these laws is because it is a place of learning, it is a school. It is different from the rest of the universe because it is a place where everything created must learn. It must learn its own control, it must learn its own responsibility. The fact is that nature, particularly in the animal world, uses its sense of responsibility in a way that the human element within man cannot tolerate: for example, the eating of its own young, especially if that young is not perfect; the different species living upon one another to provide food. Nature has its own Universal Law of balance.

This, as yet, man has not learnt and the reason why man is so slow in learning these apparently very simple and very effective laws is because of the God energy, the principle of love, which he has within him. It is born within him and is induced to grow, to become a living part of his existence through sharing, through learning, being aware that God exists, feeling the emotions of fear and love. The feeling of hunger does not usually produce the need for cannibalism and those that have in the past lived in that manner have been more innocent beings who have not yet progressed to the understanding of the sanctity and the preservation of human life.

So the basic principle within the Earth is to provide balance. This is done through the intelligence, through the sight and through the awareness that this is the inherent nature of life, whether it is an overgrown garden, whether it is a home that will no longer house the increasing family, or whether it is where decay or accumulation of dust particles begin to take over the space in which man lives. It is one of the simplest laws that exist universally and yet it is one that has taken mankind the longest possible time to begin to recognize and to use.

The fact also that, particularly with mankind, there must be a balance between positive and negative energy is another reason why the Earth is different in principle to the other planetary life, the main difference being matter. It exists in all living things upon the Earth. Without matter man cannot exist. The other ingredient, that of oxygen, is essential for all living matter upon the Earth. In fact, if oxygen is denied, even inanimate objects also begin to disintegrate and cease to exist.

Planetary beings
G: *Are you saying that man is a material being, i.e. he has a physical entity, a physical vehicle, a body, and that planetary beings do not have a physical body?*

M: That is so, as well. There is life on the planets but that life exists as a form of energy and light which does not take on anything approaching human form. Therefore humans when they step upon a planet, such as the Moon, (which is virtually the only one that man can step upon without being consumed by the different gases which are upon all the other planets), cannot see or touch or hear the life that does exist there because it is in a form which is invisible to man.

G: So is planetary life rather like the spirit spheres? Is planetary life in a sphere of its own on each individual planet so that what we perceive as a planet is perhaps its gross physical manifestation and the life that is there, is in fact, on a more subtle level, beyond a vibrational frequency that we can actually experience?

M: That is absolutely right, but don't get it muddled up with the spirit world. The spirit world as it relates to mankind surrounds the Earth. There are the seven layers or spheres in which spirit resides, and that appertains only to the Earth world. It does not appertain to any of the planets. So you must have that distinctly separate, if you are writing about it.

G: Yes, I meant merely to use this concept as an analogy rather that an actual fact. So there is no spiritual dimension on planets other that the Earth, is that what you are saying?

M: No, there is not a spiritual dimension but there is an etheric dimension.

G: And the etheric dimension, would that be what one might call the aura of the planet?

M: Very largely, yes. But it is a little more complex than that. Things on the planets do change and they do quite simply die. They are not so perfect that they keep on regenerating or even remaining in the form that man sees them currently through his telescopes. They do change and there is a form of death upon the planets but as the energy that motivates the planets into life is of a different complexity to humankind, the death is also of a different nature. So there is no need to have the spheres encircling the planets in order to contain that which has been, that which has transformed.

G: So following on from that, does that mean that in many

respects there is actually no evolution of planetary life? That planetary life just is?

M: Indeed so, it never changes. It doesn't grow as such. There is no evolution, as with man over the million or so years, from that which was very primitive. Nor yet the changes within the animal structure, as you have had for the hundreds and thousands or a million or more years of the dinosaurs, for example, which are proving to be of such great interest on Earth at the moment. There is nothing of that kind [the dinosaurs] which have transformed into much smaller species (because many of them evolved into the animals that you now have upon the Earth and whose presence you enjoy greatly). So there are no species as such in planetary life. It is purely energy, intelligent energy, which helps to keep the planets in their strict rotation.

Those who really study the planets will find that there is not one iota more or less space between the planets as they revolve. It is always the same distance absolutely and they do not change their position at all. It is the intelligent life appertaining to the orbiting planets that helps to keep them in that particular order.

We are trying to find an expression that perhaps would allow a greater understanding of exactly what this intelligence is. Forget about humankind, forget about an interrelationship of the intelligence; it is nothing like your science fiction. This intelligence does not communicate on any level except that of the awareness of its own purpose in relation to the purpose of other particles which are in or on that particular planet.

G: So if they have no matter, they are not linked to their planetary home in the same way that human beings are linked to the Earth?

M: That is so.

G: I'll move on to another question, which is related to this again. Does the soul need to experience life on other planets in order to gain knowledge?

M: There were aspects of the totality of soul which, at that stage of creation when it became manifest, were allocated to the different planets. It had to be so because soul is living energy and the different planetary life couldn't exist without soul energy. There would be nothing there for it to germinate from, to continue its life force, and it was envisioned that all the planets, including the Earth, would be there within space for billions of what are termed years, earthly years, before their existence was no longer required.

Therefore, when soul was allocated different means of progression, some of that energy went in maintaining the life force of the planets. It has its own reality, it has its own intelligence. But it is only the soul in relation to the Earth which has the second aspect of God, the love aspect, circulating within it to create emotion, to create sympathy, compassion, love, hatred, all of these very human emotions that rule man and that cause man to be what he is, a living embryo of life.

As we have explained in *The Way of Soul,* it is that energy force which enables the soul to continue throughout its long journey through existence, whereas within the planetary forces it is integral to each individual planet. It radiates around and within the planet but not beyond. There is not that loving compassion because the soul is not individual; it is not fragmented as it has been in order to enter into humanity who can give voice and experience to the soul's knowledge.

Perhaps a good way of explaining to some people is a pottage of soup. There is the one pottage; it is there, it fills the vessel, there is nothing else within it to give it any particular substance, to give it flavour, to make anyone approaching that pottage to feel, 'Oh yes, we really would like to have a spoonful of this'. If they did, it would be like taking a spoonful of water with nothing in it to flavour it or give it any substance. But as different ingredients are added, so the variety within that pottage becomes available to those who wish to taste and consume. The only difference is it never becomes less, it always maintains its level of existence within that pot but it varies as different energy forces enter it, as different commodities become important for man to aspire to and are right for him to wish to taste and to work with.

G: So our Higher Selves, we as human beings, would never actually choose to have the experience of life on another planet because that is only one aspect of the God force and we actually contain the love aspect as well? So it would be an incomplete experience as far as we are concerned?

M: Of course it is, although many modes of thought say that planetary energy is more advanced than that of the Earth. Physically it is, because the planets were created long before the Earth. They had to be finished, perfected, they had to be absolutely in accordance with the rhythm of life, otherwise the Earth could not be placed into its centre and begin to grow until eventually it would become a habitat for those particles of soul that truly needed to advance, needed to learn through action, rather than to learn through being. So when we say that the Earth is the centre of the universe, it is more in a metaphysical way than it is in a physical one.

G: I see.

M: When you look at the situation of the Earth and the planets you are seeing physical reality; you are seeing the actual situation. But you are not aware of the energy force emanating from all of those aspects of universal life, how they relate to each other, how they relate to the Earth and how they relate to the space between, which is equally important.

UFOs

G: This leads me to another question. We have a suspicion, (no more than that because these things are kept very quiet), that planetary beings visit the Earth from time to time. We have the phenomenon of UFOs and the occasional strange occurrences: people saying they have met a planetary being and so on. Do these beings somehow inhabit our physical world to do that? Do they have to physically travel from their planet or do they just manifest in whatever area they choose through some sort of mind power?

M: You see, it is not every planetary being within your universe that has the power to transform into human life, to emulate human life in any way at all and thereby to visit the planet Earth. It is only from one particular planetary source that this can take place and that particular planet, you could say, was a prototype for Earth. It knows that the Earth exists and that it needs to be disciplined, that it needs to learn very much faster than is taking place so that it doesn't create its own destruction.

Being a prototype, it is aware how long the Earth has, how much interference should be given to speed up the ability of man to use his own intelligence and how much intelligence from the planetary source and Earth source can interrelate. So a great deal of the progress, especially scientific progress, that is achieved on the Earth comes about through that interference of these planetary beings. When they transform themselves into a structure that can withstand the atmosphere of Earth, they do look not unlike earthly beings, but they have not perfected the analysis of human beings, even though they are doing this, they are experimenting on this. They are far more at home within their own form of existence. They find the human body extremely clumsy and have no use for it on their own planet.

It is these that have devised a way of living, not very far from the Earth, within the Earth's atmosphere, creating their own travel arrangements. They mostly dwell within what you call UFOs because there they are more comfortable with the body they have created, and also they are able to use the UFO to conduct their experiments. The main problem here is, and always has been, the urgency and the anxiety of these beings, (we will not call them creatures for they are not), to enable the Earth beings to hurry up their progress into something that will preserve their world.

There is another element here which, if we have time, we will discuss and that is how the Sun, with its force, plays a part in enabling the Earth, with its force, to continue to exist, to revolve in space along with all the other planetary elements. But that may have to come about at another time.

G: I shall certainly hold that in reserve at the moment, as I just wanted to pursue the planetary being part for the moment. The planetary beings that can actually come to the Earth, are they planetary beings from within our solar system or do they come from beyond it?

M: They are beyond it, which is why that particular planet, although it is moving toward the solar system, has not yet been perceived by those that study the skies and why it is that these UFOs are imagined to come from the existing planets.

The concentration of learning about these planets seems to have as its motivation the planetary beings – to be able to communicate with them and to find out their purpose within the creation principle. Of course, they don't exist on the planets, and the planetary life itself, being purely and simply energy, would not communicate with Earth. Those within the vehicles, where they can maintain a life structure and where they can come very close to the Earth, they can communicate and they do. But they haven't yet found exactly the right way to establish this communication so that those upon the Earth can communicate through language. They can only use electrical impulses toward the brain to attempt to transfer their knowledge to mankind. Sometimes it works, sometimes not, so they also are having to learn how to communicate in a way that mankind can relate to.

G: *So communication from planetary beings at the moment is like telepathy induced by electrical stimuli into the brain of man?*

M: We would say that that is very close to it, yes.

G: *You have said previously that we on Earth are intimately linked to our planet because we are made of the same materials as the planet. Therefore, by our very nature we have a crystalline structure within our cell walls as does the planet at its centre, i.e. the minerals have a crystalline structure. Now, it seems to me that mankind is a form of link, if you like, between the physical material world and the spiritual world. It is almost as if we are a kind of conduit through which spiritual energy may enter and go deep into the Earth. Is that one of the functions of man: to be able to bring down the spiritual energy to nourish the centre of the Earth?*

M: Absolutely so. That is why man is unique within his universe and he will never be able to live permanently on any other part of the universe, because his link with Earth is more than just walking on it, digging it, and being aware of its atmosphere. It is his spiritual link which is also within the Earth, he could not live in isolation on any of the planets, certainly not within a UFO, even if he was transported to the planetary existence from which they have emerged. He would simply die because there wouldn't be the stimulus, there wouldn't be the mental rapport with those beings that man must have in order to exist and multiply. His ability to regenerate himself, his ability to procreate would very soon vanish.

Energy fields around living beings
Increasingly we are becoming aware that there is an aura or energy field, which surrounds the physical body, sometimes

referred to as the subtle bodies. There is a form of photography, known as Kirlian photography, which can detect this subtle 'light' around all living things. I see it rather as you would magnetism: you have the physical magnet, the block of metal, but surrounding that there is a magnetic force field which is also an integral part of the magnet and is, in fact, its main property. Within the auric field of the human body there are energy centres, in much the same way as a magnet has its poles, and these are known as chakras. There are many of these chakras in the human body but there are seven main ones.

G: I presume also that this energy exchange that is going on all the while we are on Earth would cease if we were to exist upon another planet or in a UFO. Therefore we would not receive the nourishment from the planet because part of the way in which the structure of man evolves is through contact with that energy exchange, through the chakras and through the subtle bodies –

M: – and purely and simply through touch. The regeneration that takes place within the body through the simple power of touching one another can never be underestimated. Those infants that are kept apart in incubators, or in some countries as experiments, never being with each other, never feeling or touching a human being, simply being fed on a conveyor belt, they do not really exist as the conduits of love, of spiritual love upon the Earth. They are little automatons and they would very soon perish and die through that lack of contact, which is essential for human beings to have.

   Similarly a person living in isolation begins to lose the power to regenerate their organs and to keep themselves healthy, because there is no means of doing this without the natural impulse of touch, of love and compassion. It is something tangible, it actually moves from the body towards others. It is not something of the imagination or something that is explained only because there is no other method of explanation; it exists. It is a natural energy, which must be used as an exchange for life.

G: Returning to your point about the influence of the Sun on the life of the Earth, would you now like to elaborate upon that?

M: Well, it is not only a source of light; there is a great deal more. There again, the Sun was an initial prototype for the Earth itself, a regeneration system that however long it existed would never become less. The form of gases that comprise itself and its heat are self-generating and will always remain so. Even though there are many particles which drop away and simply go into space, where they die, it will always be there as a source of light and energy for the Earth and for all that it needs in order to enable growth.

Deep within the Earth there is exactly the same energy supply in every respect. The Earth does also contain a few other elements, which condense it, which prevent it from consuming itself and which, of course, allowed all the different strata of the Earth to adhere – everything that was able to adhere to it, as it revolved in space until, after millions and millions of years, it was prepared to be inhabited, first by vegetation, then animal life and then humanity.

It needs the Sun because it is part of the Sun, it is an aspect of the Sun that broke away at the beginning of creation and formed its own life.

The myth of Lucifer
This brought to mind the myth of Lucifer, the angel (whose name means bearer of light) who broke away from the other angels and from God and 'founded' the under-world. I wondered if there was anything in that and put the question to him on another occasion. His answer is printed at the end of this conversation.

Regeneration of human tissue
If science researched the potential for regeneration of human tissue, (for example, the growth of limbs when they have become diseased and have to be amputated), on some of the very simple aspects of nature and its own regeneration, its own ability to grow when depleted, it would very soon be possible for humankind to regrow a limb that has been amputated or to regrow its own kidney or liver or gall bladder when it has become diseased and has been removed.

It can already stem the disease through a particular form of healing, through mind power. It doesn't have to degenerate to the point of poisoning the body and thereby being removed. Although medicine has moved forward tremendously in the last

2,000 years, it has not yet reached the analysis of what enables the body to grow into a body from that first cell and emulate it, so that the cells can be encouraged to re-grow when they have had amputation.

G: Is this regeneration capability triggered by vibration, in terms of things like crystal healing? For instance, maybe an organ of the body resonates to a particular frequency and if your mind can resonate to that, or a crystal can be placed near you which resonates to that particular frequency, would that be a possible way that the trigger might work?

M: In theory it could do but, of course, once a limb has been amputated and the connecting cells have died, there is nothing there which can still draw life and produce life. That has been finished by cutting through the cells and treating them in such a way that no regrowth can take place. The crystal can help the healing, can help to stem the flow of blood, can help to repulse any decay, but in that situation it cannot promote regrowth. It can only do so if it is introduced to the area of amputation at the time it is taking place so that those cells regenerate, recognize the DNA within themselves and begin to grow once more; like some little animals do indeed grow again a limb when it has been snapped off or lost. They have that ability, it is within their capabilities, and it is within man's, if they could find the way forward to encourage it. But man is too logical, man doesn't have sufficient imagination to allow himself to experiment until he finds the way to accept that growth and encourage it.

G: It seems that really everything is vibration, that the Earth, our cells, our organs and our limbs, everything about us has a vibrational quality. The picture that I have of the way in which orderliness is maintained in the universe and the way health is maintained in the universe, (not just physical health but the health of the whole system), is through this pulsating energy from the God force, which comes out as a spiral, as you've described before, where the different colours are pulsed out. I see that we are like receptors that pick up the vibrating frequency of the pulsating energy from the God force, which then contains the blueprint or instructions for the orderliness of our lives, our cells, the maintenance of the whole system throughout the universe. Would that be a good overview of the system?

M: Yes, it is, and you could say that this pulsating energy from the God force is like a magnet to which mankind adheres. He cannot break away from it, it is as essential to his existence as are food and water. This life force from the God source is also essential to enable humankind to continue their existence. It is like a magnet attracting to man that which is of the same process within him, as is indeed the force itself coming from the centre of existence.

G: *One of the other questions that has always intrigued me is how astrology works because I see the planets as large physical objects which revolve around the Sun and yet somehow their position relative to one another creates an influence on the Earth.*

M: Oh, yes.

G: *I can see how the Moon does that with the effect on the tides but I still find it difficult to understand how, for instance, a planet like Pluto, which is way out on the edge of our solar system, can have an influence. I presume that it is not just a gravitational energy, there must be something more to it than that?*

M: Each of the planets has a particular ability, a particular power. Think for a moment of a musical scale and think of a tuning fork to which the notes have to conform in order to harmonize, to synchronize one with another. So that as you become aware of that scale of those notes, they do not jar on the system. They are in harmony with your own hearing, with your own balance within yourself, your acceptance of those notes as being within that scale and relating to the note of that tuning fork.

Each planet has its own radiation and there is an interlinking between each of the planets in the same way as there is a linking with the atom. As each atom [in a molecule] maintains its hold on all the other atoms within the chain which are essential to the integrity of its molecular structure, and which give the structure its properties or characteristics, so the planetary systems are held together with this same atomic force. Very fine links exist between each one so that they do not move out of their synchronicity and they do not move any further away from the Earth than was designated when they first existed. If anything happened within this fine web of atomic energy, which is the actual universal structure, then everything would fall in upon itself as if it were entering a black hole and disappearing.

So each one has a relationship with the one that is next to it on either side. Each planet has a particular note within that vibration, within that frequency, which relates to the tuning fork which is the Sun. That is very, very oversimplified but it may help understanding.

The Aum and the music of the spheres

The Aum or Om, as it is sometimes referred to, is the universal mantra chanted by mystics of many faiths down through the ages. The Master frequently refers to the significance of the Aum and it is well known in Buddhist, Hindu and Tibetan cultures. It has been described by the enlightened as the sound of the universe. It is said that it may be heard in places of great quietness, such as those remote mountain retreats where mystics choose to dwell in isolation. Under such refined conditions it is possible to become acutely aware of the sound of creation, as the perception and awareness heighten.

And it is more than just relating. How do you think the notes of music ever became part of man's existence? They existed within the universe long, long before the world did and long before man was developed upon his world. It is part of the universal sound, it is part of that Aum and the Aum itself is like an atomic unit. It holds within its universe everything within its power. There is always a relationship between the sound of the universe and all of that which exists within it. Each was given its meaning when it was created and because of this it cannot change. There is nothing in existence in man's world that could defy that structure or allow it to be destroyed in any way at all.

So these beings that exist within the universe to relate to man, to create a harmony between man and the other planetary existences within its universe, they could not dwell on any other of these planets. It would be impossible because the structure that they harmonize with is too close to the structure of humanity. If it were not so they could not relate to humanity. They also relate to that cell on the planetary structures which resonates with the beings within those UFOs and that stretches out beyond your universe into deep black space. But it is gradually moving toward the universe so that it will eventually be seen. There will eventually be the kind of communication that man is seeking. Man will need this, it will be important for his own survival – not that man is going to live upon it. Man has his own spiritual spheres which, when his life is complete, he returns to. It is simply that the Earth would for a while become a void with no humanity upon it. It would then regenerate, largely with the help of these planetary beings with their far greater knowledge and ability.

We spoke some while ago about the need of these beings to communicate with man and how they wish to colonize the Earth, because their first love, you might say, is of the Earth and its survival. It is not emotional, in the way that man relates to his Earth, but a knowing that the Earth is essential to the universe and therefore these beings relate to it through that form of emotion, their intelligence. We felt that if they colonized the Earth before it was absolutely essential for its survival, that they would simply eliminate man, deciding that he was hopeless at creating and abiding by Universal Law or keeping his Earth moving and regenerating as it should.

It is essential that they do not come, that they are not allowed to be provoked into coming to the Earth, even invited here. And they will not be, all the while there is the existence of the powers of good and the Masters of Light and everything that conforms to the rhythm of the universe. They will have to do their part in what is considered to be their role. So many of these experiences mankind has of being in these vehicles, seeing these creatures working on and with them, they do exist in fact, although it is that part of man's brain that relates to his subconscious which throws up these visions, throws up these memories and they simply appear to be fragments of imagination. Does any of this make sense to you, my son?

G: *Yes it does. I can see the need for rebalancing and I imagine that man, as he is currently, is not really in a position to be motivated to do very much about it. It seems to me that the powers that be at the moment are content to pay lip service to that kind of concern but not actually to engage in a proper solution. So I can see that an influence from beings of a higher knowledge would be what would be necessary to restore a balance.*

M: But it should not occur for a very, very long time. Certainly not during the life of man as he is today.

G: *It strikes me that space is a very cold place and we know from very low temperature physics that when the temperature is down to almost absolute zero, energy transfers are free from resistance. In other words energy transfers are very much more efficient. I just wondered whether many of the energies that we have been discussing actually travel vast distances across the universe because of the fact that the universe is at a cold temperature and therefore resistance is very much decreased?*

M: That is so. That is also why it is that when man is extremely ill and certain very technical operations need to be done upon him, it is far better to reduce his temperature until he is virtually no longer living in order for him to survive the very deep surgery that is undertaken.

Man does relate to absolutely everything within his universe but there are, of course, many ways in which that relationship can come about and each way doesn't happen at the same time. It is a very gradual deliberate knowledge that comes about as time passes to which man can then relate and expand upon and make use of. So without science, without those with the ability to relate to the God force in order to bring about the scientific knowledge and evidence, it would be impossible for man's growth to continue. This is why we find it so extraordinary that the very beings who have the God force and its structure in the palm of their hands are the very last to accept it and recognize it. Do you not find it so, my son?

G: *Yes, I think that the problem is that there is a polarization between the head and the heart. Many people who are very intelligent, very committed to seeking the truth cannot accept values on the heart level and therefore miss very much more knowledge than they would ever dream possible. So they continue almost with just one eye open rather than looking through both eyes and coming into harmony with the truth.*

M: When they eventually accept that there is a mind that controls all these things, they will then also accept what actually allowed them to bring a computer into existence within the world at this time, just as it is vital to the existence and survival of the world to have such an instrument. If they can relate their computer to the mind of God, they would then have the answer to everything.

Our time with you is now complete, my son. We look forward to the next time, to your questions and our ability to find an answer to them.

G: I will look forward to it too.

M: Till then, my son, farewell. Shalom.

G: Farewell, Master. Shalom.

✡

The myth of Lucifer
During a subsequent conversation I decided to return to the subject of the myth of Lucifer.

G: You've mentioned that the Sun and the planet where UFOs come from were both prototypes for the Earth and there is this rather interesting story of Lucifer. Lucifer the light bearer moved away from the God force into other realms, and I wondered whether the story of Lucifer was a metaphor for the Earth breaking away from the Sun?

M: He has got rather a bad reputation, poor chap, has he not? Referred to as the fallen angel, banished from the court of God – which, of course, is all the talk of ancient times with their belief in what God must be, and the realm of God, because people at that time were unable to relate to anything except their own humanity and what they could do and what they could suffer or create. Absolutely everything, including the concept of a fallen angel, had to be related back to themselves.

It is interesting that this is brought home so greatly in Egyptian architecture. When they looked upon the god Ra, they were looking upon one who they felt had not only the energy of the Sun within him but also reflected the purpose of the creative God in his humanitarian side, when he actually lived upon the Earth – both of which were far from reality, from the truth of existence.

Lucifer represents the negative aspects of everything within existence. God is supposed to reflect all that is worthy, all that is a positive creation – in other words, light and the manifestation of light. Lucifer is meant to represent darkness, innocent darkness, night-time, all the dark things, the dark energies which seem to come alive within that period upon the Earth when shadow is cast upon it – and that truly is all it is.

There is no devil that has a fiery furnace of torture and everlasting damnation to the soul. What there is is the ability of the soul, once released from the human body, to see the reality and the truth of every movement, motion and thought that went through the body during its lifetime on Earth, whether it was the ability to hate, to be cruel, to destroy life or whether it was the desire within for the very opposite, for the creation, for the love of humanity and compassion. Most of mankind hovers between the two, so they go to the first sphere of life after death. No recriminations, just seeing clearly what the reality of their life has been. But there are those who have manifestly throughout their lives sought to destroy, to kill, to gain power.

Now the devil, Lucifer, whatever you might like to refer to him as, is also representative of power, power that destroys, power that strangles, that is truly overriding the freedom that God has given to man with his free will. So both God and the devil are, in their true reality, the good, the evil, the positive, the negative, of all aspects within creation. But you try and explain that to some people who say that they are haunted by the devil or that the devil has done this, that or the other to them. Man's acceptance depends so often on his early teaching in youth and particularly the teaching of the church.

G: It is interesting that Lucifer's name means the bearer of light; it's as if he has a name which his reputation doesn't substantiate.

M: Well, yes, that is often the case, is it not? But looked at in that way, he can be the bearer of light in allowing people to see the darker side of their souls, the darker side of reality. He can bring the enlightenment that is needed to draw them toward the God force, toward that which is good and positive within life. So it is not a misnomer really, it is just that he has got muddled up with the figure of the devil, the horned beast.

Chapter 8

Conversation Seven

*The Big Bang. Atlantis. World War II. The God force. Man's
relationship with machines. Values for the future. Earthly power.
Core values. Aum Shekinah.*

M: Welcome, my son. Shalom.

G: Welcome, Master. Shalom.

The Big Bang
Science has managed to probe back into pre-history and
can now define the stages of the violent origins of our universe to a minute fraction of a second before the event
known as the Big Bang occurred. It was from this point
that the physical universe was born and also time and space.
I wondered whether the spirit spheres, which are beyond
time and space, were also created at one and the same time
or did spirit pre-date the Big Bang?

*Note: In his answer, the Master uses the description 'Big Bang' to
refer, not to the physical beginnings of our universe, but to the
'explosion' or fragmentation of soul which created individual souls
or Higher Selves. This, as he indicates here, took place at a much
later stage, when the world was already formed and inhabited by
animals and primitive man.*

The Big Bang and the spirit spheres
*G: I'd like to continue on from our last discussion in which we
talked about the planets. Your teaching, and I think science also
confirms this, is that there was a Big Bang and from that event not
only flowed the material world but also I presume at the same time
the spiritual world became manifest at one and the same time. Is
that correct?*

M: Not absolutely. The cycle of events was that the planets had
been created, they were all in situ, and the soul was still one
mass of energy field. The world was gradually developing
which, as you realize, took many millions of years, slowly going
through many stages to become the area of vegetation that was
needed for man.

When that had been achieved, and when the animal kingdom had reigned for possibly another million or so years ... we are thinking mostly of the enormous creatures, the dinosaurs. Incidentally, this was very important at the time because being such vast creatures, when they died and decomposed they gave a great benefit to the Earth. They left behind many of the necessary minerals, bone products and so forth that were feeding the soil and allowing those areas of land – and there was still a great mass of water – to flourish even more. Where the enormous fish were concerned, because very little of this we feel has been touched upon even scientifically, they did also feed the waters and the land beneath the waters. So it was a very important part of the evolutionary scale.

Now when that was complete – and there were many hundreds, even thousands, of years where the world was overcoming the effects of the comet that destroyed the dinosaurs – then there was a great deal of awareness amongst the soul energy that very soon it would be necessary for more objectivity, more very necessary spiritual work to be done but in an individual pattern. Man began to develop from a near-animal species – but, as we have pointed out so often, there were always the differences, the size of the brain, the ability of coordination, there was always that difference, but there was not the link with the divine. This came in with the Big Bang, with the soul fragmenting and very gradually as it came into the individual humans, so the response to divinity, the free will, the freedom of choice, the ability of the brain to coordinate with spirit began to take place. So it was another stage, you see; it was after the dinosaurs, it was after the great quietness, we would call it. Probably that which is referred to in the Torah regarding the silence over the Earth. That happened after the comet. Is this beginning to put it more in its sequence?

G: *Yes it is.*

Atlantis

Atlantis has always been something of a puzzle for me: a great civilization which existed on the Earth for many thousands of years and yet we find no artefacts, no remnants of its presence. There have, over time, been many attempts to discover its geographical location and to link it with later civilizations, which followed in the wake of

Atlantis and Lemuria, another fabled early civilization. There is speculation that Egyptian and South American civilizations arose from the Atlantean influence whereas the Asian civilizations arose from the influence of Lemuria. The Master teaches that whilst the Atlantean civilization used crystal energies, they did not have the physical link with planet Earth as we do. We are comprised of matter, the same matter as the Earth. Indeed, as science has discovered, the cells of our bodies are made in part of liquid crystals which resonate with the structure of the Earth.

G: As I understand it from a talk which you gave just recently regarding Atlantis ... Have I got it right that the Atlanteans were actually different from humankind today because humankind have something of the element of the planet within their make-up, because they have some sort of crystalline relationship with the planet, which the Atlanteans did not. Is that correct?

M: That is very much so. A completely different species, completely different timescale and indeed a parallel world. But as is the way of parallel worlds, they so often interact, so you could put the Atlantean period upon the Earth down as that which would be a prototype for man as time passed. To see the relationship of man's species with the beautiful crystals within the Earth and also their ability to harmonize with the beings of light who they could communicate with, who were able to come to the Earth to teach and share. It was indeed a time, we suppose you could call it, of God's imagination being able to succeed to a very great extent, with all the wonders of nature, with all the wonders of the crystal world and the ability of humankind to use them, to make the most of them. But even at that time there was this almost total disbelief that man could engender such evil in order to succeed. So the Adam and Eve story of the good and evil fighting each other was very much part of the Atlantean period.

We have spoken of the Eldars – or Els, as they were also known – and how the civilization that evolved from the blending between the Els and humanity gave birth to a rather rarer civilization of people who had the best of both worlds. They were partly aware of a far more spiritual way of life and the essence of life within them. Whereas those that were early primitive man would have had very little of this, they would have had far more matter within them. But it was a necessary form of progression to bring into the Earth a higher existence from the other planes of life. Otherwise there would always have been a separation between the spiritual spheres and the Earth's essence, because life on Earth was evolving slowly over millions of years with its own progression from insect into animal, from animal toward human and so forth.

So the Atlanteans were a civilization of humanity, of people, but they also related to the other spiritual spheres in a way that humanity has never done since. Mankind is now beginning to reawaken to an awareness of those spheres through teaching, through the acceptance of the wisdom of the Lords of Light and the Teachers of Light in a way that certainly would not have been possible before 2,000 years ago, because there was virtually no contact, metaphysically speaking.

Egypt began the contact with these priests that were able to travel in their sleep state and bring back wonderful information from these other realms. Since then that contact has ceased to develop, has disappeared, and other ways have had to be found [such as this present method of channelling through a medium]. But the Atlanteans were human beings with a link to the spiritual forces which had been proved to them in an irrefutable way which man, modern man, has always found difficult to relate to.

G: I see.

M: Of course, the civilization is there and so much has been attributed to other later civilizations. They do have their roots in what the Atlanteans had when they occupied most of the earthly world, other than the oceans. Where so many historical buildings and wonderful edifices have been discovered at extreme ends of the earth, man has thought, 'How did that architecture get from here to over there and with all those oceans and apparently no contact between the civilizations?' Yet the remains of an elephant is found in one and a tiger in another and they don't realize, as we've been trying to explain with another series of talks [yet to be published] on the formation of the continents, how much ocean there was, how much land there was and how the plates of the Earth shifted. It is so difficult to see or imagine anything other than what is present now in today's reality.

G: Yes, I can see the dilemma that man has today because he does imagine that Earth has had this kind of format for all of the civilization of present man and therefore any great change in the format of the oceans and the configuration of the land would seem to be something that happened well before the time of man almost.

M: Of course, specific architecture relating to a particular culture has its own very special style which thinking man has to accept related to the civilization that created it, wherever in the world it might be found, whether buried or at the top of a high hill or mountain. The same thinking, the same culture, was behind that creation.

G: I think there are certain historians now who are beginning to make these connections. They are still rather discredited in terms of the academic archaeological investigations but these ideas are now beginning to be published.

You teach that, at a certain point near the end of Atlantean civilization, a decision was made to follow the path of the negative rather than that of the positive. Bearing in mind your teaching on parallel universes, I wonder whether in actual fact a parallel universe had opened up at this point in which the positive path had predominated?

M: Oh yes.

G: So did that parallel universe go on to greater things?

M: At some time we really will have to go into this very, very deeply, will we not? Most of the parallel universes, when they come into existence, come about because of conflict, which is usually the reason for them. Sometimes they go on to a certain point for thousands or a million or so years and then they come to an end and that is finished.

For example, the universe which showed the Nazis were the victors of the last world war, that parallel universe allowed that particular evil to wear itself out. It went from bad to worse until the atomic bomb blew up so much of the world that the parallel world no longer existed. Now, this would have happened with the world in which you live, which is the really important world for learning, for everything that is taking place, everything that is working toward perfection. When it gets to the point where humankind can no longer cope with the negativity that is spreading, then a parallel universe opens out to receive it and in it goes.

Then there is a period of time where things are a great deal calmer, a great deal better. Taking that period of time at the end of World War Two, possibly for the next 25 years, it was a time of recovery, but there was great harmony. It was quite amazing really. If only humankind hadn't been so greedy again and wanted so much advancement and to take, take, take, that could have gone on for the 50 or so years that have transpired. But they didn't, they wanted more. There was the Cold War, which was a period of peace, and then after that all the negative energies began once more to assert themselves. So man is just about ready for another parallel world we feel. But we do hope that the period of time that the Archangel Michael reigns, with his wonderful energy, and with the Children of Light coming in, that this might be avoided. [The new age we have just entered, the Golden or Aquarian Age, is ruled over by Archangel Michael.]

Negative aspects of free will
G: It is certainly true that there does seem to be an element in humankind – and I think this is particularly true of those who dominate society – that a certain amount of self-interest, to the detriment of all others, seems to creep in to the decisions and to the system of government that we all labour under. We are therefore almost coerced into a state of submissiveness and acquiescence in the growth of values which maybe are not in the best interests of the positive, the best interests of the light.

M: That is so apparent at this time, and unfortunately the world seems to be on a merry-go-round of events, none of them really achieving very much. If a country or even a continent does show signs of more harmony, something seems to happen to create disharmony within that situation which again spreads. We have to recognize that it is the free will that does this and if anything happened to really destroy the free will – and it was very close to happening during the height of World War Two – then that would have meant that the purpose of man no longer existed.

Incidentally, some of these parallel worlds have eventually merged into spheres of light, especially where there have been those that are very pure and where man has really understood his purpose.

The relationship between parallel universes and free will

G: I am aware that in the spirit spheres there is no time. I was wondering whether the parallel universes that have been created in the past are in some way fixed but those that are yet to form, are they moving and shifting according to events and according to the play of free will?

M: Yes. What is happening upon your Earth here in your experience is constantly shifting and changing. You have only to look back about fifty years where the last break into a parallel world occurred, which took on the extremes of what might have happened had the results of the war gone a different way, allowing this particular world to go forward with a greater sense of freedom and of right. Now, those two worlds, yours and the parallel, had absolute extremes of life emerging from the one conflict.

G: Would I be right in thinking that the governing mechanism for these parallel universes would in fact be something like the planetary alignments which would bring influences to bear on each of the parallel universes so that they do in fact come back into some kind of alignment?

M: That is very often its purpose. That is so and, of course, there has recently been one.

G: Yes, I see, so in a way that is almost like the controlling mechanism whereby the parallel universes either spawn or reabsorb one another so that the whole thing moves forward, rather like keeping something in time, like a metronome.

M: Very similar and, of course, you can also use this analogy when you are thinking about weapons of war. You can take, for example, the atomic bomb and all these terrible weapons which are so destructive in their power that they could at any time wipe out humanity. The world itself would take so long to recover that life would virtually cease, and what life was left would not be worth the existence of humanity and the rebirth of other soul aspects.

A parallel universe might be formed under such circumstances and, of course, it is the Masters of Light that have jurisdiction over what is taking place. It is they that decide whether this takes place in the world of experience which you are all living on, or whether a parallel existence is formed to work out some world karma, or whether it is purely and simply a rebalancing of positive and negative energies to enable man to see more clearly what is taking place within his universe and to enable his progression to start again on a more equal footing.

G: Am I right in thinking that, as we move through what we call time, that the universe actually goes into a process almost like cell division where new universes split off and either die away or merge with the light as they then develop? It is almost as if we are an engine house for this process to occur.

M: That is an excellent way to put it, my son. Put that way people could understand the expression 'parallel world' or 'universe' so much more clearly. It is the same process but different words of explanation.

G: Yes, I have a feeling that what is happening in the process of time moving forward is that it is like the evolutionary process of the creative principle of the God force. I have this strange, almost quirky, idea that in fact what is happening is that God is recreating himself from a sort of cell-division process. In other words, infinity is becoming more infinite as time goes on.

M: God is indeed a cell of energy that does keep on expanding, retracting, expanding again, and with each expansion and the obvious retraction that must come from that, then that force is one step further into evolution, one step further away from the very primitive beginnings of the universe – of this world's universe, shall we say? Because there are so many universes beyond the one that man is aware of, which you can call the parallel worlds. But the God force is there also, because the God force is pure energy and nothing survives without energy.

G: Would it be true to say that before the God force expands into the space available, there is a kind of chaos and then as that harmony, as that intelligence, as that creative principle expands into that new area, that new structures arise and that the spirals and the sacred geometry of creation begin to assert themselves over what might be a sort of randomness?

M: Yes, yes and it is that God energy – for want of a better expression, which we constantly seek – it is that God energy which provides the sacred geometry over the power of chaos.

So many things within existence are a struggle: the struggle of good and evil; the struggle of life over death; the struggle even within the spheres of light, which extend around the Earth, to give the Earth its ability for infinite expansion and growth – because it is not the Earth of many millions of years ago, it is a greatly expanded Earth and many, many of these spheres that surround it are indeed fragments of the parallel worlds that have been created from these constant battles.

Without humankind and its ability to grow, to relive itself within its young, without that, nothing that has occurred through this period of time could ever have left behind that which man can learn from, that which he can relate to. It would all be separate particles that were existing in their own gravitational field, unable to communicate, unable even to be conscious. It is the consciousness that man receives from the God force that gives him the ability within his life pattern to adapt to circumstances, to be aware of what others around him are feeling, expressing, giving vent to.

This sets man so completely apart from the insect world, which moves in coordination only because of the instinct of the separate species. Those who see ants at work see an intelligence there. But it is not an intelligence such as that which the God force gives to humankind through His own consciousness and His own ability to share that consciousness so widely with the human species. It is an instinctive 'being-together' occupying what is taking place within those ants. They have no minds, they have no intellect; they are purely an instinctive force doing what is necessary, as part of all the processes of the insect world, to promote healthy earth. Does this make sense, my son?

G: Yes, I think what I'm beginning to understand is that the animal kingdom operates within a typecast role in which each species and each individual in a community – of insects, for instance – plays their part. However man, because he is an expression of the love principle of the creative force, needs to have free will and the two actually go together. You cannot have the love princi-

ple without free will because, in fact, what you would have to do is come into what I would call spontaneous right action freely, of your own choosing. Otherwise you become as mindless as the instinctive behaviour of the insect world.

M: Indeed yes. Of course, from time to time as man is seeking his own eclipse through concentrating on building machines that will take over his function, that is a great and very serious worry to the Masters of Light, who keep a watching brief on what is taking place on the Earth.

They see these huge machines taking over like robots, like ants within their nest doing things automatically, providing functions to which man, because he has his free will, cannot respond, and with which he cannot live, because that kind of environmental condition is right outside man's comprehension; the species would be eradicated. It would take a while to do it but eradicated it would be. Machines have no soul; machines have no heart or consciousness, no ability to relate to the suffering of others. They purely and simply act out their function the way they have been programmed. The ants have been programmed to work for the Earth; robots are programmed as the servants of man. But if man himself gives robots the right to become the masters, and man becomes the servant, then his species will be eradicated.

The perils of man's relationship with machines
G: That's a very sobering thought, Master, because I do indeed feel that the vast majority of people today serve machines. Machines do not serve the creative principles of human beings and it is very apparent at the moment that people are being observed, monitored and assessed for the contribution that they make toward the mechanical world and to the vast corporate bodies in whose interests these machines exist. I think that is why there are so many people who are in such dire straits and find it difficult to survive, either financially or spiritually.

M: That is very much so, very much so. When you think that within this last century there have been those who have been so close to the spiritual realms, with their ability to be influenced by the forces of the angels and by the Spiritual Teachers, that they have witnessed in their minds what could happen if this began to be so. They have warned of it, they have written of it.

They have preached the warnings which those in charge of the countries do not heed. Then we are indeed very, very sad that man walks toward his destruction in the way that he does. He did it in Atlantean times; it was the survival of the fittest. It was spirit moving in toward the end of that great era that allowed those with greater vision to overcome and to escape.
We really do not want any of this to reoccur in the new millennium. We really do not. Where would man escape to now? What part of the world is still fresh and virgin to allow him to be able to set up once more his life and start again? All right, there are vast areas of countries such as Australia that have been untapped in respect of their resources. You could say that this could house a few million people but in reality it just isn't possible. Not now. It might have been a million years ago, or even 100,000 years ago, but not now.

G: This begs the question, as ordinary human beings how do we proceed from here? We have an almost inevitable march of progress towards this destruction. How do ordinary people respond to the energies of the time in a positive way and how can we actually change things to move forward?

M: Unfortunately the destruction, once it has gained momentum, will continue. This has been brought about largely by man's mismanagement of his Earth over a very long period of time. There has been damage done to such things as seams beneath the Earth's surface which is giving rise to these dreadful landslides and earthquakes which are now very prevalent in certain parts of the world. There will be the destruction of land and, of course, the destruction of humanity with it because it is so sudden and man is not concentrating on being aware of when an earthquake is likely to occur and so does not evacuate those within its perimeter. He is concentrating rather on further destruction, due to the weapons, due even to the foods that he has created, let alone the fertilizers that have been developed.

All of these things are very small when they start but they soon begin to escalate so that they become out of control. It does need a very firm hand, with governments that can see into the future, that can visualize the results of the actions of the now – which, of course, will happen with the Children of Light. We have already explained this but there are still many years to pass before they are old enough, strong enough, and free enough to be able to make themselves heard. So the destruction will continue, probably for another decade and then, very gradually, the population of the world will begin to diminish as people's knowledge of how to prevent, not just the birth of future generations, but the creation by unnatural means of future generations, all of which is so utterly unnecessary and which is viewed from a spiritual viewpoint as being, once more, the tools of destruction that man himself is creating.

Enduring values for the future

G: *So to put it in the context of the creation story of Adam and Eve and the snake and apple, we are very much at the point of the dilemma where, having bitten the apple, we are grappling with the snake of free will and the apple of knowledge.*

M: Yes, and that will continue until the influence of those such as the Children of Light begins to be felt. They will utilize law and utilize their strength in order to overpower those in authority who are quite willing to view destruction, very aware that they will not be present in life to suffer the ultimate results of what they begin. It is this inhumanity within man that saddens us: 'Whatever I do, I don't know who comes after me, so why should I worry if it profits me now? Then so be it.' It is this attitude that the Childern of Light will not allow.

G: *Yes, I'm afraid that is very much the motto of the last decade. There is a lot of short-termism and opportunism, irrespective of the consequences of whatever actions they may take. I'm sure that in terms of spiritual law, of course, these souls who undertake these decisions which are so momentous presumably then come back to experience the consequences of their actions. So in many respects they do actually feel the effects of their actions but not necessarily in that personality in that lifetime.*

M: They should, of course, be more aware of the principles of reincarnation but the church certainly doesn't help them with this. Certain aspects of religion are totally against the idea and even if you look to the beliefs outside of the Christian church, they might believe in the reincarnation of animals into people, or people returning as animals if they do not correspond to life in a genuine way, but that doesn't help either because it is not the truth and people think, 'Well, if I can escape the consequences of my actions by coming back as a much-loved little cat, then so be it.'

Of course, it doesn't work like that, so the more teachings such as our own which are echoed by so many other teachers throughout the world from the spirit realms, the more those listening talk about the reality of reincarnation, the reality of coming back to experience what has been initiated in a previous life, the less likely man is to perpetrate these disasters and make these agonizing decisions which result in the demise of other human beings. Would you deliberately set an atom bomb upon a whole country, if you realized fully what the reaction on your soul, on its ability to go forward into enlightenment, was going to be? Of course you wouldn't, and those who instigate these actions are seldom people with any particular spiritual belief. They are usually people with a great deal of agnosticism within their make-up. 'When I'm dead, I'm dead. That is the finish.' 'Do what thou wilt' is the whole of their law.

Earthly power
G: Yes, I think that is very much reflected in science in terms of Darwinian evolution. One is encouraged to believe there that you just exist for a period of time, you pass on your genetic structure to the next generation and they then move forward. It is interesting that if we all wholeheartedly adopted that particular philosophy, then the way in which those people behave is, perhaps the inevitable consequence of that want of a depth of knowledge, beyond just the physical world and the mere nuts and bolts of evolution.

M: Of course, so much that is drawn into the consciousness through a way of life is passed on through genetics. It doesn't take a lot of imagination to point the finger at many different countries within the world to see the way, even in the last few generations, or the last two or three centuries, that this is presented. When you see the instigators of the very bloody wars that have taken place, they come from the centre of particular countries or continents, which have this inbred within them.

Right-thinking people, people from gentle countries, are absolutely horrified at the licence being given to these other very powerful countries which seem at the moment to be benign, to be benevolent. But then as soon as they get sufficient power around them, then mankind will see what they are capable of doing. The old biblical expression of the third and fourth generations – it is so true. All things do pass through those generations and we are now coming into the third generation since the last world war and already man is seeing what those countries are capable of, in quite a small way. In the fourth generation the power will be unleashed. So, of course, we had to bring in the Children of Light. They are infiltrating into those countries slowly but surely, so we hope that in another 20 years matters will change. If they do not, then everything we fear will come about. The people of today, the people in power today, just shrug their shoulders: 'Oh well, if it does happen, at least I won't be here.'

G: It is interesting that the way in which power, political and earthly power, is asserted these days appears in some way to be benign, to be acting in everybody's interests and yet what is then introduced is something which is restrictive and curtailing the freedoms of even the most ordinary people. We can see this in many of the wars which are occurring around the Earth at the moment where we are encouraged to believe that the bombings and the shootings and the armies' presence is in some way to do with maintaining the rule of government and the rule of law in countries which are lawless. But, in fact, the very means by which these countries go about asserting their authority can be much more crude and brutal than the original problems in those countries.

M: Of course. These countries that are having the assertion placed upon them, those are the countries that are endeavouring to look back into their past, to learn from it, to live more simply. They are not the creators of the mechanical world. They are trying to preserve their Earth, their way of life, the way that they farm, and the way that they bring up their children with values. But there are still those of overpowering strength that wish to defy nature and destroy those who could be the salvation of nature and of the Earth.

Lifestyle values
G: It is certainly true that even within the developed world there are organizations like the Green Party, Greenpeace and other activists who wish to halt this spread of technology into those areas where technology has no business. They are very much marginalized and put on the fringe. In the media in particular they are portrayed as people who are not quite respectable. It is very inter-

esting to see the way in which publicity and the propaganda is so phrased that anyone who offers protest somehow or other must have some other motive or agenda which is not respectable.

There is a principle, formulated some 40-50 years ago, called the Gaia Principle which invests the Earth with a consciousness of its own. This allows it to transform and to bring about its own healing, irrespective of what happens on it. Is that principle, or something like it, true?

M: That is our teaching, my son, very much so. We try to allow this to filter through many of the different subjects that we teach that people are interested in. We don't always give things the accepted name that they have become known by, but, yes, the principle of the Earth regenerating is absolutely so.

The principle of man regenerating is also a fact. But so often man does not assist in his own regeneration because of his way of thought, his fixation with degeneration and ultimate death, and also, of course, his way of life, very often the food that is eaten and the circumstances he surrounds himself with. Generally speaking, people in the primitive countries lead a much healthier and much longer life if they are allowed to get on with the process of living in a way they understand. It is the intervention of these so-called powerful and forward-thinking countries that usually ends in the destruction of that which is more primitive but is, in many ways, much closer to the Earth and closer to God and the God force, even if they do not know consciously to what they are relating .

Until man does go back in his process of regeneration to appreciating what he had during certain periods of life, until this occurs, his prospects for surviving what lies ahead and the process within it are very fragile indeed. Certainly the kind of periods we do not wish to see again would be those of 300-600 years ago. That was a time which could well be eradicated from the history of the future. To go back to that would be to completely destroy everything man has learnt in the last 200 years. One hundred years ago man was well on the way towards a good survival, towards an appreciation of his Earth and then the wars of attrition began.

G: I think that the decline of order at that time stemmed from the First World War. A great many people who were very highly evolved, very self-sacrificing, lost their lives in that awful conflict.

M: Indeed. Nearly all of them are now back on Earth, well equipped with the knowledge within them of where countries and rulers went wrong at that time. It is their voices that are so against the voices of so-called progress which are taking place in the various governments of the countries of today. They are opposing the spread of armaments, they are opposing nuclear warfare. If only they could be really listened to and not put down as being inadequate people who don't know what they are talking about, if more would listen to them, then the Earth would benefit very greatly from their input.

Core values

G: I feel that we have lost our core values, our ethics and our integrity along the way – certainly in the last 30-50 years, it would seem to me. The time was very different when I was a child. There was a sense of right and wrong, whereas now it is almost an anarchic way of being and living.

M: People were reaping the benefits then of the survival of good over evil. But it doesn't stay potent within the minds of man very long and greed takes over.

We are not against people having things; we encourage it. We feel that people who have around them things they treasure, things they prize, give a great deal to society in the way of appreciation and in the way of love and hope for the future. In general it is those that shrug their shoulders and say, 'Nothing really has a value', it is those people to be afraid of, not those that treasure what is theirs.

G: Following on from what we've been talking about, obviously the Earth meditations that we do at the time of the full and new moon are very important to this process of realigning the planet with its own regeneration. Presumably this also encourages humanity to come into alignment with what is positive and good.

M: Oh yes.

G: So if we were to start meditation groups and specifically do Earth-healing meditations on a very regular basis with a lot of people, would that transform the situation?

M: It would go a great deal toward transforming it, yes. So also if the Aum and the Shekinah are incorporated within the period of meditation, even from time to time coming in with two or three very slowly, very gently in the middle of different levels of meditation. This helps the ability of the sounds to penetrate into the layers of the Earth which respond to those sounds. [See Appendix II]

The meaning of the Shekinah [a Hebrew word also meaning 'to reside'] is to be able to bring the Christos into the personality's life, to blend it so that the true soul aspect of the Christos and the soul aspect within the self merge together. They become a light within, which can then be shared, subconsciously or consciously, by those who use the mantra with others they mix with, work with, or have their friendships with.

So what is important with the Aum Shekinah is the resonance of the sound. The sound is a pure golden sound, very high resonance, a resonance that immediately goes above that of the world's awareness and into the spiritual. The more that it is repeated, the more powerful it is – as indeed happens when the twelve Aums and Shekinahs are sounded in the rhythm of a group, imagining that the sound is going around the group and round again, linking and bringing out all the colours of the individuals, merging it with that beautiful golden colour of the sound itself until a spiral is formed, and within that spiral there is again even more of the spiritual connotation being drawn very deeply into the awareness of self. You could say spirit linking with matter and bringing about transformation as it does so, bringing a very deep awareness of peace within the chanter, within those who can perhaps visualize, be aware of colour and be aware of sound linking with colour in order to create balance.

G: *I think this might form the basis of our talk next time, if we could focus on sound and its importance in the creative principle.*

M: We would enjoy that, my son. We would enjoy doing that very much indeed.

Chapter 9

Conversation Eight

The sound of the planets. Geometry and cycles. Parallel universes.

M: Welcome, my son. Shalom.

G: *Welcome, Master. Shalom. We were going to cover sound, today. Because this is such a vast subject, I would like to give you an open floor. What I will do is interject with questions as they arise from this. I have done a lot of work on sacred geometry and things like the Fibonacci numbers [a series of numbers which describes natural forms], the cycles of thirteen and seven and so on. I do appreciate that this is actually linked to the thirteen notes in the musical scale and also that the planets and our Sun, the universe itself, has a sound, so I would like to open the floor to you now to give me your views of sound as a creative process.*

M: We will enjoy this, as we do with all your subjects, of course. We would like to start with that universal sound as it relates to man's scientific discoveries.

The sound of the planets

There has been much conjecture recently regarding the lack of sound coming from Mars. Apparently, some of the instruments that have been specially prepared and sent on the Mars expedition into space are very, very sensitive and it was hoped that the sound of Mars itself, the vibration of Mars, could be contained within these instruments and sent back to Earth. There was great disappointment when it was found to be silent. Several suggestions have been put forward, some of them sensible, many complete nonsense. One of the suggestions was that the machine was burnt up in the atmosphere on its way through to Mars itself. That cannot be so as there is not the same kind of atmosphere as surrounds the world that man lives in.

What does not seem to have even been considered by scientists working on this project is that they have based their instrument on sounds that have already been heard, already been discovered. We gave a throwaway comment recently that space is one of the noisiest places imaginable, and space *is*. Those who are travelling through space pick up the most amazing noises and sounds as they travel. But when they actually get to their destination they find it is a very different story. Those who reach the Moon and who have walked upon its surface commented upon the extreme quiet that resided there – a little like being in the middle of the Antarctic with nothing but snow surrounding you, deadening any vibration that might come from the centre of the Earth. It would indeed need very precise instruments to relate that central energy of the world to the sensitive human ear.

Where Mars is concerned, it *has* a vibration which may have been recorded by those instruments, if they were only able to interpret that silence. Special dog whistles will attract an animal from miles away but the human ear cannot pick it up. An animal might very well pick up the sound from Mars but how can an animal translate it or enable its human owner to relate to it? It cannot. So, where they say there is no sound coming from Mars, there is nothing that they can *interpret* as a sound and, of course, it is possible that the instruments are not sensitive enough for that particular sound to be relayed. We would hazard a guess that they are; it is simply that man has nothing sensitive enough in his equipment to show there is a sound that is available.

So that starts us off with all the different planets. They all have their identification, they have their signature and that signature is a certain sound on a scale. Now, my son, how many known planets are there within your solar system?

G: *I think there are ten known planets, also lots of moons.*

M: How does thirteen sound to you?

The sound of our solar system
G: *I would think that logically thirteen would be the right number, because there do seem to be thirteen notes in the scale.*

M: Each of those planets has a signature note making up the harmonic scale. If you then allow for all the vibrations between to make that sound melodious, harmonious with all its tones and half tones that flow in between to make an absolute awareness, that is the planetary harmony. As each of those planets is eventually invaded by Earth life, even if it is only with their instruments going toward them, some sound will be perceived by the human ear, some will not.

Of course, there is a great deal more to it than just a harmonic sound but if we start from there then maybe science will begin to relate to how to hear it, how to understand it and why it is that planets revolve with such precision and why they are unable to shift their axis in any way at all that is going to fundamentally cause the Earth to waver in its mission for as long as it is needed.

G: I would think that thirteen planets is probably the right number in the sense that –

M: They are not all known about yet.

G: – this would be in line with the natural progression of the Fibonacci numbers, which are also related to spiral forms. So would I be right in thinking that the sum total of the sounds from the various planets in our solar system actually produces a scale which could produce a sound approaching the Aum?

M: It is the Aum.

G: I thought this sound might have some relationship to this. In this respect the number thirteen seems to be a very important number for a lot of creation. It is the seventh number of the Fibonacci series. It is this series which defines many of the growth patterns of plants and animals, and even segments within things like ammonites, spirals and shells and so on. Does the number thirteen have a particularly significant role to play in things such as sacred geometry?

M: It does. In mythology, it is accepted that there were thirteen Deys, or Eldars, that were assisting God in his creation of the universe and that when this had been completed there were seven Deys or Eldars that were then working with God on the minute details of life as it was to emerge, in order that eventually animals and man could exist on the Earth in harmony and assist the Earth in its maintenance. So you've got the thirteen and the seven there. But very largely mythology only refers to the seven Deys – not meaning seven days of the week at all. It was seven Deys with the hierarchical structure of energies that assisted God.

Seven- and thirteen-year cycles

G: *We also see these cycles in what we see as the passage of time. Throughout our lives it almost seems that every seven years something happens, something changes, a vibration, an energy in our life process seems to change.*

M: Very true.

G: *Is there a thirteen-year cycle as well? Is that another important cycle in our lives?*

M: Yes, because, for example, from birth to thirteen, puberty commences. We consider the true majority in, when people become fully mature, is 26 and so forth. Then you've got old age and the approximate date of demise for the great majority of people. All of this is still in thirteen-year cycles.

G: *We have always thought that over a cycle of seven years all the cells within the body will have been renewed. Some cells last longer, others shorter, but over a period of seven years our entire bodies have actually been replaced.*

M: That is true.

Cycles and health

G: *So if we take ourselves back in our lives to a particular incident that happened, say, fifteen to twenty years ago, is it true to say that really we are a completely different physical entity now than twenty years ago, so therefore the influence of that past event is not really anything other than a memory now? Or does it reside in the physiology?*

M: It does reside in the physiology, but nothing resides exclusively in the structural memory and, of course, there isn't complete rejuvenation of the cells every seven years. There is change, but it isn't rejuvenation. There is a different structure that is evolved during that time. Most illnesses which are accepted into the body during that period of time have either evolved so that the recipient has passed on or it has simply moved out of the structure and is no longer relevant. It might be there as an echo. Somebody born with a heart defect isn't going suddenly, miraculously, to lose it in the seventh year. But it will change its structure and the physiological growth of that individual will have accepted its presence and the rhythm of the body will continue bearing that in mind. So maybe by the fourteenth year it will either have terminated that person's life, or it will no longer be a threat and so it continues.

G: *Yes, you've anticipated my line of questioning here, because I was thinking that there are certain cases where people had life-threatening diseases, such as cancer and that kind of illness, which is a purely regenerative process which seems to have gone wrong. Yet sometimes, miraculously, the whole sign of the illness and the signature of its presence do actually completely disappear.*

M: Yes.

G: *It would seem to me that there is a way that perhaps the mind, or that the cycle of seven years, enables the slate to be wiped clean at some point during that cycle, if we could but access it.*

M: It is the accessing of it that is the most difficult because of man's incredulity. If science could focus on this a little more and maybe monitor a number of people, then they might find that they are making sense out of what many feel to be fiction.

G: *It occurs to me that perhaps a certain kind of vibrational influence at the right point in the cycle may well be the kind of medicine of the future, whereby a particular life-threatening illness could actually be diminished just by a very non-invasive type of treatment at a point in the seven-year cycle.*

M: That is very relevant.

Note: **At this point, the conversation moved on to subject matter which was outside the range of topics to be included in this book. As is the way with these gently meandering conversations, we never did return to the subject of sound. Instead I chose to clear up an area of questioning which had arisen from previous conversations, returning to the subject of parallel worlds.**

G: *Now, as a final point, you have mentioned in the book that it is what happens here in this particular reality that is of vital* *importance. I think we have come up with the idea that the reason why so much attention is being focused upon us is because we have strayed slightly from the script, as it were. We are holding things back and we need to catch up. I just wondered what is the lesson of this particular reality that we currently exist in, and whether there are composites, like a positive aspect of this and a negative aspect, which actually come together? As I understand it, what we are dealing with here is the conflict element of creation.*

M: Indeed yes. We would not have explained it or described it in quite the way you have but we understand the concept, we understand what it is that you are seeking to understand. As you know we always like to make analogies so that mankind can see clearly and understand, from the human point of view rather than in the abstract. So if we use that, hopefully it will help.

G: *That's fine, Master.*

M: The simple way to put it is through the concept of the mother. The mother contains within herself everything that is needed for conception and giving birth, for passing on her own DNA, and then after union she gives birth. What her offspring receives is partly of her knowledge, wisdom and being and partly from another source – that which is coming through the father. But the children are imperfect from the point of view of the mother.

Now, if you will lay this concept a little to one side, let us look at the concept of parallel worlds. The world in which you live was a prototype; it was conceived and born from the perfection of God's knowledge, His wisdom, which has been created as nature. Man with his ability to relate to the God force, to that wisdom, is within nature and responsible for nature's growth, responsible for the reaction of everything that takes place in the Earth. So the Earth is the mother, Mother Earth, the feminine world. All actions which are done in the name of God, in the name of Mother Earth and the ability to preserve the Earth for man to live upon, results in offspring. It results in something which man himself desires to perfect but he has to make do with second best, hoping that within those offspring there will be something that can relate to the mother, with the perfection that the mother has.

So you have got the Earth, which is the main world, it is

the structure upon which everything is conceived. Then you have got your parallel worlds, which are the offspring, which are the result of actions, misconceptions or even, in some cases, a quality which cannot exist in a world of conflicting views, conflicting actions, conflicting thoughts – something which is too perfect. There wouldn't be enough contrast for man to survive very long; the idealism is too narrowing.

Take the parallel world that was created at the end of the last world war. There was an idealism there within the reason for the conflict. There was the ideological desire for perfection, especially perfection within the creation of humanity, the perfect race. But anything that becomes too perfect becomes very flawed. In creating a world where there was the parallel to the victory – in itself imperfect but much closer to the main structure of life and what is required to come from life and through life – that parallel world led to its own destruction because everything that was impure was destroyed. This meant that there was no impurity, or so-called waste, that could provide nourishment for the Earth and for man. Who is to do the menial tasks? Who is to clean the sewers, for example – a college professor? Therefore, over a period of some three or four generations the light burnt out. There was nothing to generate growth. There was nothing to provide the positive and negative from which growth must emerge, so it just faded into oblivion, an empty world devoid of life. The planet was neglected because everyone was seeking so much perfection that it was too menial a task to plough and hoe.

G: *Yes, I can see what you are saying, because it is the diversity that creates the variability. The universe is the unity of the diversity, isn't it? So it moves forward. What appears to happen is that this particular world is the engine house, so to speak, for the creation of the positive and negative aspects which produce corresponding parallel universes as spin-offs, whilst this reality moves forward as a harmonizing of the two opposites.*

M: And everything else is a little bit, in the vernacular of the present, rather like cloning. It was very much cloning that went on in the parallel world of the victorious Third Reich. In fact within that parallel they discovered and worked with cloning before this world in which you live, (this prototype world actually came upon it scientifically with its possibilities so very recently), and they more or less perfected it. The human mother was no longer needed except to produce that which was the ultimate perfection until in the end she was unable to produce. She had been perfected out of existence.

G: *I see, yes. You can equate it with what is happening in our country today, where those people who till the land and those who produce the tools we actually need to survive are being ignored at this present time, to the point where they are being written out of the equation, in terms of our life in society. It is very much the same kind of thing, on a different level, isn't it?*

M: Of course, if you begin to think of the world of cloning that is already taking place, with these fertilized implants. They are fertilized outside of the womb to be as perfect as possible, making sure that all the imperfections that the soul needs and desires to experience because of karma, all of that is scientifically got rid of and this perfect embryo is implanted to grow, to produce what? Almost a mindless spiritual-less clone who in time will not be able to contribute what the world needs to sustain it. So there will be another breakdown. In other words, another parallel world will be created through the scientific so-called experiments in perfection. So that, on the one hand we will have once more the world that reverts back to the aims of nature and the necessary imperfections that humanity and nature together produce. On the other hand there will be another world of clones but of course differently orientated from that of the Third Reich parallel world.

It is complex. Nobody can understand it to its full maturity because the imagination runs riot and the whole concept of parallel worlds as they genuinely are is very new. There was a lot of information on parallel worlds given to less experienced mediums over the last 30 or 40 years which were really the fruits of the imaginations of earlier teachers. A different form of mediumship and channelling has now developed, where the Spiritual Teachers can actually directly formulate the knowledge that they have and speak it through their mediums. Then the truth can be expressed. So there is more knowledge, more acceptable knowledge and the kind of knowledge that is factual and is the truth. A lot that took place earlier in the century, or even after that war, can now be ignored as being just a first attempt at a process that has now been perfected.

G: *Yes, there is an interesting analogy with what you are saying about parallel universes when you look, for instance, at the breeding of pedigree dogs as opposed to mongrel dogs. You very often find that pedigree dogs suffer far more in the way of ill health –*

M: Indeed they do.

G: *– whereas a mongrel tends to have a bit of character and a bit of spirit and is rather cheeky but actually very robust.*

M: Much more loveable.

G: *I find that so, yes. And now, Master, I am sorry to say that our time has run out.*

M: Then we will say farewell, my son, until the next time. Shalom.

Conclusions

The Millennium. Spiritual values. The middle road. Overcoming fear. Learning from nature.

During the course of producing this book, I developed a very strong opinion about the nature of life today in the material world. It is my belief that, as idividuals, we have to engage fully in the process of life. I feel we all need to free ourselves from the addictive trappings and conditioning of the commercial world to embrace a much broader range of experience and to grow in wisdom and awareness. For so long many of us have pursued the mirage of style over substance, not wanting to awaken from the dream and own the problem. All the while the Earth and the environment have paid the price for the want of sustainable, enlightened and holistic solutions.

I see our future as dependent on a change of attitude and a new awakening of the awareness of our connectedness, not only with one another but also recognizing the symbiotic relationship with the Earth itself. We need to accept that we should not manipulate, control and abuse one another but love, accept and share the gift of the Earth in a harmonious way so that the ailing planet, upon whose bounty we all depend, can regenerate and recover from the complacency and ignorance of modern man.

I care about these issues very deeply but perhaps run the risk of being called an idealist. I decided to discuss this with the Master, in order to frame conclusions in their proper context, based upon our discussions and incorporating both the material and spiritual perspective.

M: My son, shalom and welcome.

G: Welcome, Master. Shalom.

M: We always look forward to these conversations that we have with you and as they become less frequent, as the book develops and takes shape, we look forward even more keenly to these sessions. So we won't waste a moment of this time with you. Do proceed with your questions, my son.

G: I was going to write a conclusions section myself and then it occurred to me that maybe we could do this together in the spirit of cooperation. I can give you some idea of what I got from the book and from my conversations with you and, for your part, you can tell me where the core of the material lies and what you would like people to take away from reading this book. Perhaps you can indicate the way forward for mankind from the present situation that we are faced with.

M: It sounds excellent. We are sure that we will come to a satisfactory blending of ideas and truth within the context of the book itself.

The Millennium

The year 2000 was an anomaly in that it represented the changeover from the Piscean to the Aquarian Age in the minds of mankind, whereas the true boundary is 2001. In order to accommodate the expectations of mankind the energy transitions began during the year 2000. There were successive bursts of energy from spirit: a large burst at the winter solstice 1999, and again at the spring equinox and summer solstice 2000, with a much smaller burst at the autumn equinox 2000, which from a cosmic perspective completed the energy transition into the new age.

The Star of Hope is the brightest star in the sky, called Sirius, and appears on the southern horizon in the northern hemisphere. Sirius was utilized by the Masters of Light for channelling a special energy towards the Earth during the closing years of the century. The Master calls this the Star of Hope because it signifies the hope for the new age in so much as the spiritual values of life will now come to more prominence than has been previously the case. In time it will be replaced by the advent of a new star, which the Master refers to as the Millennium Star. It is truly a symbol of hope for our continued spiritual evolution.

Man is still on the threshold of the new millennium, 2000 being a year that doesn't really exist in the annals of time. It is just a year where at different specific intervals universal energy has been channelled into the Earth – largely through the Star of Hope – to enable man to adjust to the energy changes in a more harmonious way than if he had plunged straight into a very different understanding of life than he had had earlier, while the Piscean Age still reigned supreme.

One of the things that is happening is that people are being faced with issues and those issues are very challenging because they are on a very deep level. They are not issues which are very cut and dried: should I live here or should I live there? Should I have this job or the other job? They are issues of principle, of dogma, of spirituality and the best way forward. There are far more of these issues emerging and, as each burst of energy comes towards all of you, it enables the mind to function, the brain to function and a greater clarity to emerge from a chaotic scene.

G: Yes, I take what you say, because I, too, have been through my challenges, and people that I know are being challenged in this way. I hope this book may well help others towards an understanding of the process they are in. There are many who are being individually challenged on various aspects of their deeply held beliefs, the way in which they live, or the value systems that they have. My hope is that they can take solace from the knowledge that this is a cosmic process, that they are in a period of transition and nothing will remain the same. Perhaps then they will be able to look with hope, with love and compassion towards one another and not begin to sink into despondency or a lack of faith in the future –

M: – and fear regarding the past, which has entered into the consciousness of some people. We would say that the changes have been telescoped into the past fifteen to twenty years and have been indicating the way forward and moving everyone gently in that direction. But this year [2000] has been a year to pause, to think, to look back, to project forward, and the year to come is that definite movement forward on the path, which is a path of truth. If this is reflected within the book as a whole, or even in this little section that you are seeking to put together, this will bring clarity to people as to why they have encountered their problems and dissentions. It will bring confidence that they are equal to the challenge and worthy of that path which they are about to step upon.

G: It seems to me that it is very much a time of letting go, of being at ease with the process of letting go. Maybe it is a time for shedding those things which have become familiar in the landscape of one's life but in actual fact have prevented one from fulfilling one's soul purpose –

M: – been holding you back.

G: Yes. It does seem to me that the freedom and the advantage that we enjoy in our society today – due in no small part to our scientific and technological advancements – have a converse side in that they have held people into a very rigid structure, whether they know it or not. They cannot be spontaneous, they cannot just allow themselves or others to change in the way that perhaps in more primitive societies one could do without very much of an upset in one's life. Whereas what we now often find is an intolerance towards those who wish to adopt an alternative lifestyle, outside the norm, and a kind of repression of those values because they are different. I feel that can be quite dangerous in the world today.

M: The spiritual values are gradually coming forward as people relinquish their desperate hold on the religious values and dogma which have prevailed for many hundreds of years. It has come to a peak within the last decade, a peak where people have sought that inner comfort that once religion truly brought to man. By religion we are not only speaking of the Christian religion or the Jewish religion, or the Moslem, but all the many other quite rigid beliefs that have prevailed for many hundreds and thousands of years.

In a way, many people have almost reverted to paganism, certainly to becoming agnostics, because they have feared the church or come to fear it. They found that the leaders of the church, those that propagate the religious texts that have been written, have feet of clay. They, too, are human but others have revered them; they put them on to pedestals and have not allowed them to step down to walk among them.

This is what Yeshua did. He walked among man. He was one with them, He suffered with them. He went hungry and cold with them. He showed them by His integrity, by the way He felt and wished to share. He allowed them to see His inner self which was pure, which was unsullied by man's sin. He approached man's sin not to decry it or deplore it but to enable him to see how it can be changed, set aside and how the true beauty of life can be acceptable to all.

It has been very, very important to recognize this again

within the last few years. It is so important to lay this dogma to one side, to bring about a spiritual awareness which is not attached to any particular religion and yet reflects all religions in certain little rituals, certain quotes, beliefs and actions. This will be the way forward, this will be the way of the future and in the next few years this is what man will begin to absorb and all men will walk together. You have seen the terrible uprisings between Moslem and Jew [in Jerusalem]; you have seen the same between the Serbs and the Croats, between the Christians and the Moslems. This had to happen; it had to be part of the cleansing. The cleansing of the past decade and the progress of this year will be reflected in the years to come.

G: It seems to me to be reflected in the way in which we elect and choose our leaders, in business and politics and government. They also have become remote and very attached to what might be called political dogma, and business dogma, so that they do not appear to share the same kind of life experience that ordinary people live. It does seem to me that if mankind is to move forward in any kind of harmonious way into the new age, then there has to be a change of heart and mind at the very top.

M: Of course, that very top, as you referred to it, will in the fullness of time be filled by the Children of Light. The purpose of their entry into mankind, their progression through being made aware of pure teaching and life as it truly is, will be very important for the next stage in their growth. As they become more mature they will fill all these important areas of life and bring a new, a very different awareness and quality of life. Another 20 years will see them in all these high offices and then you will see how everything will change, but there have to be all these steps along the way. Nobody can jump from one side of a bridge to the other without falling short and plunging into the ravine, and that sets everybody back.

G: So what would be the way forward for the rest of us? I rather suspect most people are in many respects innocent; they live their lives in a very matter-of-fact and down-to-earth way, not touched by the need to go out and amass power or wealth for its own sake in the way that some of the political and business leaders seem to. Nonetheless we are all affected by these changes and therefore what would our part in them be?

M: An awareness of what is taking place supposedly on their behalf. You can take what is happening all over the world at the present time as indicative of the changes that are being instigated by common people. They suddenly realize that they are suffering at the hands of those that have and they don't want to be have-nots. They have thoughts, feelings, humanity stirring within them and they want what others appear to have with very little effort because their leaders call upon powers that they themselves are not prepared to call upon or do not have the ability to call upon.

It will be very much the middle road. It will promote the ability of mankind to live in harmony together because they won't be stirred up all the time by those that seize power by grabbing it from others, in order that discipline is imposed by the few on the many. Most of these powerful people are afraid of man until they realize that they have nothing to fear as long as they share and as long as they allow man's free will a reasonable expression. He can worship where he wishes, he can take his children and his family anywhere without the fear of being shot, once those in power realize that man, common man, is not there to disrupt the organization of society.

Man wants organization, he wants rules and regulations, providing they are fair. It is like children at school; if they are given permission not to work, to disrupt, to do whatever they wish to do instead of following a routine, then a riot takes place and nothing is achieved. Those same children will study quite happily and amicably and want to learn if they are disciplined in a gentle and loving way. This is the way forward and this will gradually become more apparent, both to those that lead and those that follow.

It is all within the teaching that is included within this book. There is a hierarchy, it comes down from the source which is all-powerful and yet all-loving, through the different areas of government until eventually it is those who reach up for that truth and guidance that receive it, welcome it and allow their being to be immersed within it. There must be a hierarchy; without it there is always anarchy.

G: One of the things I feel is that science has advanced from very primitive beginnings to the position of being able to understand and manipulate the world in which we live today. By and large this is for man's benefit but there does seem to be an emphasis on the acquisition of knowledge but not the means to gain the wisdom to use that knowledge. At the moment we have the possibility of power without responsibility. That can be anything from somebody who has the possession of a very sophisticated hi-fi system and plays it at full volume to the detriment of the neighbours to something like a multinational corporation which wants to damage the environment for some sort of commercial gain. It seems to me that what you have been saying in the book is that one needs to look at how wise our actions are and how we actually acquire knowledge with the necessary wisdom alongside it.

M: Man has been searching for this since the beginning of applied intelligence in the branch of humanity which developed from the extremely primitive status of early man. You can compare primitive man with the embryo within the womb. It has all the potential, every cell is in place to develop and grow until eventually it is there to sustain life and to walk upon the earth but that doesn't give it wisdom; it only gives it the where-withal to be able to develop and to absorb wisdom.

One of the very important aspects of mankind is his ability to choose, to see a way forward that will stabilize his life and give him quality. Animals with their power of instinct cannot do this. As the centuries have passed, as the ages have come and gone, the quality within those ages have helped to bring man forward, to stabilize him. In some ages different forms of energy and intelligence have been generated; in others, man's growth has been monitored, it has not been allowed to gallop forward before man has developed the ability to control it.

So when you look back to neolithic man and to all these different species of humanity which are now being literally unearthed and explored, you see why it is that it is happening at this time. The technology is there, science has provided this. Science has always been not so much full of imagination as full of the ability to be able to put A and B together to make it C, and make it understand logic and progression. What it needs now, and what we see for the future, is the harmony of spiritual experience weaving in with this logic and, with this, the ability to understand technology more greatly. It has always been the missing ingredient.

Religion cannot and has not been able to provide this because religion is another form of science; it is something that has been generated as a power over man. Man views his religion with fear, both forms of fear: that of real fearfulness of harm coming to him through the wrath of God if he is disobedient; and also the fear which is respect or reverence. But many people can respect too greatly which prevents their ability to share, to be able to discuss theories in case they bring the wrath of a greater power, a greater knowledge down upon them to make them look foolish.

The way forward is clear to us: allow the spiritual to weave in like a gentle essence, one which is powerful but gentle within that power. Allow man to be recognized as a subtle human being who feels pain and acknowledges pain. In that way the whole species will go forward. It will regain what earlier man had, before the last hundred thousand or so years. There were civilizations before which had achieved a similar state, but they had not achieved it sufficiently to lay aside the power of fear. What we are seeing for the future is the power of fear eradicated, so there will be harmony. All men will understand the rights of the rest of the world to have their own belief, their own way of life, their own approach to life. They may not accept it, in as much as they emulate it, but they will accept it as being the way that those countries have evolved and want to live their lives. This process is slow, but not as slow in the next hundred years as it has been in the last thousand.

We said recently that in the future there will be as much achieved in fifty years as was previously achieved in a century. Therefore man's intellect must keep pace with that awareness; he must accept what is being relayed to him through his spiritual body, through his soul, in order to be able to enjoy the preparation, accept the change and not always be fearful of it.

G: I feel that part of the message of this book is that the spiritual awakening of mankind will also awaken him to his responsibilities toward the Earth and the realization of his connection with it.

M: Indeed so, indeed so, the two go hand in hand, do they not?

G: They certainly do, yes.

M: If you have a sense of well-being within yourself, you want to contribute this into the lives of others and the only way that this can really be achieved is in the situation in which man finds himself, in living from the land and what it produces, otherwise there is no quality. What is a sense of beauty? Is it not by seeing beauty all around? Not that produced by artificial means but that produced by nature, the subtle but beautiful blending of colour which resonates within the aura of mankind himself.

He is part of nature, an integral part. He walks separately, he has motion, he has conscious thought whereas passive nature does not. But there is much he can learn from that passivity. He can learn to accept and once man accepts the very nature of the seasons, he will begin to find a peacefulness within himself that he equates at this time only with the animal world and with the world of nature itself. He must learn to adapt, to lose some of these advantages that modern science has provided in order to regain health and regain peace of mind and longevity.

But now we feel slight conflict within, as our channel desires to diverge from us. So with deep regret, as we are thoroughly enjoying our conversation, we will say goodbye to you, farewell and enfold you, as always, with our love, and hope it will not be too long before we can speak again.

G: *I will speak to you soon. Farewell.*

M: Farewell, Shalom.

G: *Shalom.*

Appendix I

The Aum. Creation. Spirit. Universal Law. The Solar Logos and the 'I am'. The spirit spheres. The Higher Self and the Christos. Lessons of the Soul. Karma. Free will. Light streams. The aura. The aura and the body. The chakras. The single cell. Evolution of Animals and man. Time. The illusion of time. The spiral of time. A learning process. Atlantis. The Children of Light. Rays and archangels. The legacy of the Piscean Age.

Extracts from the Master's teachings
The Master has been giving teachings to public and private groups for a period of over 25 years. What follows here are short extracts from these teachings, which provide a basic framework of knowledge upon which the conversations in this book are based.

The Aum
If you can visualize the beginning of time, there was but a void. Within that void was silence, deep, penetrating silence such as mankind cannot be aware of within his world, for to man even the air you breathe has sound and movement. Within this silent void there moved a thought; that thought came from what we refer to as the Creator, the Absolute, and you think of as God – God the Father, not the Son, and yet both are one. You also are one with them, for all mankind is one integral whole. You manifest as individuals, but you share that sense of oneness which comes from the beginning of time. This sound, this movement of energy that is thought, began and moved across the silent void. At first it was a gentle sound, barely discernible within the ether. The sound was that which you know as the Aum. Very gently it began, and then the volume increased until all that existed was vibrating to this sound.

Already there were those within this void who had life, pure life – life which comes from total knowledge, the understanding of law, Universal Law, that of love. It is a special form of love that man is not capable of when in the flesh, a total expansion of giving, having and blending, a love that is not selfish and cannot bear ill will, because a negative vibration is unknown within that sphere; it is the blending of harmony, of light, of colour.

This Aum spread, and as it came into contact with various elements of matter, and also of nuclei, protons, neutrons – all these essences which breed within space – it curled its sound around them, it made them whole and individual movements within themselves, creating the planets, the stars, the galaxies. It moved on and these beings of light that you know as the Archangels moved silently with it, touching the planetary essences, creating colour and movement within them, creating a wholeness that moved within light in total harmony and structure. And when all the planetary life was formed, moving within its allocated space, they then moved silently toward another void, and that void was to become the Earth.

Creation (from another teaching)

At the very beginning of time, there was a void. Everything was total darkness, and into that darkness there came a mind. This mind was total, complete energy, and this mind spread the energy throughout the universe, bringing with it light. Into that light there also infiltrated sound. After many, many millions of years this energy began to form a nucleus that was known as a soul, the inner dwelling of the mind. At this point we would like to point out that the mind and the brain are separate entities. Even the scientific world is not sure what the mind consists of. It is such an intricate thing, belonging not only to the individual, but to all the universe also. This mind received the nucleus called soul, and again millions of years later, the soul began to split into fragments, and these fragments were individual souls.

During this time the universe was being created, and these souls were to be used to populate part of the universe, which you know as your world. It is only this world, the Earth, that souls inhabit. Eventually, these individual atoms or souls took up residence on the face of the Earth. Some took the form of animal life, some plant and eventually some human. The Great Mind or the Absolute, as we refer to this intelligence, had decided that the world would be a beautiful place, suitable for the inhabitation of all life to live in harmony together, and to create one with another their own species. The mineral and the animal life were given instinct; the soul within them was aware of their function and they kept to it and very largely, except for human interference, they still do. But the soul which was to become man was given that little extra something, which is known as intelligence, and the free will to make decisions, using this intelligence. Eventually the world was populated as the Great Absolute, the Mind, the Creator had intended.

Many people have asked us the question, why if there is such a wonderful being creating us, why does He allow such destruction and devastation to occur over the face of the Earth. Firstly, this mind is not a 'He' or a 'She' but a universal intelligence which, as we have just explained, is not capable of creating evil. It is the free will of the human being using this intelligence in his own way whose actions can create disharmony and what is generally known as evil intent.

Spirit

Pause and consider what this means to mankind: in this one action [of creation] everything which is in the world as you know it today came into being. This is what is meant by there being nothing that is past, nothing that is future. It is all here in the present. At this one burst of energy into this void was born spirit. Spirit is life – life eternal. There can be no end to this spirit; there can only be 'the now'. Through millions of years this energy pulsated, spirit became more and more aware, and gradually little particles of energy, molecules, moved away and became separated; and within this separation was the kernel of mankind, that which is known as the soul, that which is the integral part of mankind.

Universal Law

The Creator, who we refer to as the Solar Logos, did not create law. Law was and is, and is a state of being. The Solar Logos is law. That law has always been and can never be altered because the whole universe moves and has its being within its structure. These laws were created to enable the planetary system to move in harmony within the universe and for the world to take its part within this universal structure. To move away from this natural law is to create not just disharmony among men but among the planetary systems also.

As you learn the meaning of the lessons of life, confusion can often arise. You may feel that when we refer to spiritual law we are referring to those lessons you learn as the soul returns time and again from the spirit realms to the Earth world and back again to spirit. They are interwoven, but are not basically anything to do with spiritual [universal] law.

The Solar Logos and the 'I am'

The Logos is pure energy and spirit and does not need to reason, for it is, and in this state of being dwells within what is known as the 'I am', the eternity, that which always was and always will be. The finite mind of man finds it increasingly difficult to assimilate these truths but as the Aquarian Age progresses and more and more knowledge is released to the atmosphere, man's strength and understanding will grow and ultimately there will be changes, and those who return to a later life, having spent some time in the spheres, will better understand the things we try and tell you during these talks. Understanding spiritual law comes slowly, over the course of time.

We remember when we spoke before on the subject of time, we mentioned the Logos as the central pivot, out of which come all the spirals of energy and knowledge which go round and round the universe. As man is in the pathway of these energies so he will receive to himself that which is right for his development at any given time. He cannot move from that station in life, he may be receptive and desire further knowledge but until the spiral of knowledge has reached him in a further pattern of evolution he will not understand. Therefore, my children, those things you find difficult to assimilate now, you will truly understand at a later time. Think back to the beginning of your development before you had any understanding of spiritual truth, how sad you felt, how alone, how lacking in enterprise and belief, and yet now, some years on, those things we say are acceptable; you understand them; you can picture, each in your own way, those things we speak of.

The spirit spheres

When you pass from your physical body, the moment of transition from life to death is usually pleasant. It is like waking up from a pleasant, dreamless sleep in a different environment from the one where you laid yourself to rest. You are always met by someone in spirit who has loved you – not necessarily from this particular incarnation, (for there are many who feel they have been loved by none, or have given love to no one) but possibly from another life. Always you are recognized and greeted with eager anticipation; and from thence you move away with the speed of light to whatever place in the spheres of spirit that you have earned for yourself during your earthly sojourn.

We feel that there is comparatively little known regarding the spirit spheres ... There are three of these initial levels, and they are all very similar to the earthly states, except that there is nothing to destroy, no death of any kind. Life is maintained in all aspects – the duplication of the flowers and trees and grass, remaining ever-colourful or green – all these things the soul must be aware of as it is educated into the life of spirit. The time spent in these realms depends upon the education of the mind during life, but during this stay within these spheres the soul is taken to where the Akashic Records are kept. These are the volumes of life, and for each soul there is one volume, large or small, depending upon the kind of life and accumulative lives led, depending on the karma and the acknowledgement of such. The whole of that life passes before the mind of the soul. It is aware, not just of its own actions, its own thoughts, its own beliefs, but this record will be stopped from time to time when parts of the crises of life are made aware, and the soul will see the effects its words have had on others, or its actions. Again we cannot say how long this period lasts. By your standards it might be many hours, or many months, and those who wish to get in touch with the soul, in order to prove its survival, may find this waiting time arduous; but not the soul – the soul is beginning to understand what it is to live!

If the soul is well developed in its mental process of spirituality, it soon leaves these three realms and continues then in the astral plane. By this time it is well aware that it is mind within an etheric being. It has no need to use its limbs to walk, or to eat or sleep, or any of the essential things of Earth. It can project itself at will, it can be with whom it wishes. It can also project its mind back to the Earth's surface, to be aware of those left behind, be aware of the grief – even on some occasions to be present at the funeral! Your own feelings, my children, at this time, are so important for the soul. To grieve too much, too long, too greatly for the human presence, can make the soul return its thoughts to you so often that it cannot continue its life and development.

There are, on this astral plane, such wonderful things. We have already spoken of the Halls of Learning, and within these portals there is no lengthy trying to learn with the brain. Whatever the soul desires to learn is assimilated instantly, and all the opportunities missed during life for the attainment of knowledge can now be assimilated and enjoyed. Those who desire to learn to play an instrument can do so, and those who desire to write a book can find the words and the language.

It is a wonderful world, the astral plane, and we must tell you of the beautiful concerts that are there, how all the musicians will meet in a hall so vast that your mind cannot conceive it, and the audience will arrive, summoned by thought that this concert will begin. When the music rises, it is so beautiful to behold, for each note vibrates to its own colour. In your earthly world you are aware only of the sound, and not of the colour, but on the astral plane there are the colours, rising in sheets of beautiful hues and enfolding the audience in clouds of harmony. Beautiful shades of pink and rose will rise together and mingle with the colours of the music, evoking the love one feels for another, and also the love of compassion. There are, my children, so many aspects of wonder within that realm that we can only try to stimulate your imagination and your appreciation of these things.

Ultimately this realm recedes. There comes the time when the soul no longer desires to go to the Earth world. It feels its lessons are learned and that it will now achieve more by travelling to the higher spheres. The next stage is the causal plane. The soul must be prepared to lose the etheric self, no longer to be aware of earthly contacts. At this time, it is a time of decision, for there is only going forward and no returning. They enter the portals, where the light is so strong that only those who are able to achieve great heights of learning can pass beyond it and be absorbed into the light. Those who are not ready go back, but those who deserve the causal plane, those who can be the Masters and the Teachers, will go forward and will be absorbed into the light.

Beyond this plane, my children, we have no words, for we who speak to you and dwell within this plane, only know of the wonders of the higher realms, because once we ourselves are absorbed into the brighter light, we will not be able to return to this plane to speak to you of the wonders that we have discovered and enjoyed.

The causal plane is the plane of reality. It is the plane of all truth, all knowledge, all understanding – the culmination of the visual, of all the incarnations, the composite whole, where the soul understands itself and its part in life.

Beyond the plane of the mind is the plane of Nirvana, and there the soul is no longer an individual spark of light, but it is absorbed into the whole of light and energy. It is part of the cosmic system, all identity has gone and it is aware no longer of being, but of the cosmic mind itself vibrating. The love is unbelievable. And beyond that, my children, is the ultimate reality of Truth, whence we could not return and tell you one thing; but once this state has been obtained, then there is no longer any desire to return.

We will now bring you back, very briefly, to a soul that has achieved the astral plane and has been turned back from the light of the causal, having been told that there are still lessons in life to learn. This soul will discuss these matters with other minds and with the Masters and helpers within the realms of light, and from there will be taken to the edge of life, will view the planet Earth and will make the decision – where shall we return, and how, and when, to whom, and why?

The Higher Self and the Christos
We wish to describe the Higher Self, for many, desiring to picture it, find it difficult. The mind confines even energy to a small visual capacity. The soul cannot be seen in that measure. If you could see your own Higher Self at this moment, it would fill the night sky from one horizon to another, as far as our eye can travel. Beyond is a blaze of colour, pulsing energy, light drifting in and out of each facet of design and colour; and yet there is room for the countless millions who dwell on the Earth, for the spiritual realms are beyond all comparison or thought.

It is difficult to describe the spheres of light, for those aspects of soul within you who have dwelt there are blinded when they return to Earth and relate only to what they see and what is experienced by the senses given to man. Each Higher Self is different from the next, and each aspect of soul within the body is different from fellow man, (as also are the features, the figure and everything to do with mankind). However alike you may be within your family, you are still different, and the aspect of soul within you is different also.

Within those spirit spheres there are new seeds growing and they relate to those upon the Earth in the same way as man relates to man. Each seedling soul is different, is alive with love and is alive with the Christos, which did not begin with the birth of Jesus, but was merely conducted through Him to mankind in a positive way that could be manifested in the flesh. For the Christos is the seed of Life and Love, and none of these things can be separated. That which is within you in life remains in what you call death and spreads throughout the universe as one beam of wondrous light. It makes no difference if man is evil or good; the same light dwells within. It is just that the light is covered, as with a mantle, in those that will not open their hearts and minds to the reality of truth; but a mantle can be lifted, and light can shine forth and become greater. There are literally none within the Earth who do not have the potential of understanding life in its truest form.

Lessons of the soul

The soul, when it is born, has within it the knowledge of all truth, all intelligence, but it is like a locked door. It is like a student endeavouring to learn his trade, aware only of his briefest function, and having to learn all the detail, all the diagrams and sketches, the logarithms, everything which he needs to know in order to become efficient in his trade. He is prepared to study hard, to make sacrifices. He knows the journey along the way will not be easy, but when he has achieved the position, and fulfilment is his, then he can rejoice in the years of toil well spent. But should he give up this trade before he is efficient, always within himself he will feel that loss, and wish that he had been able to stay the course.

So it is with the soul; the key to all knowledge is turned in the lock when, with eager anticipation, the soul sets out on life's journey, knowing it will take many lifetimes of effort and non-understanding of purpose before the ultimate achievement is met. The main lessons the soul must learn in life are patience and love, achievement and tolerance. Much is accomplished in these things, and none of the lessons are easily learnt.

Karma

Karma is an ancient term, and one that many eastern religions commonly use, but those of you who have studied progression in life will be aware of it. It simply means 'cause and effect'. Everything within the world and within the solar system itself has a cause and effect, which means that everything that is done has its ultimate effect, for either good or bad.

It is not just the small deeds that are done in a lifetime which matter to the soul; it is the energy evoked in making these decisions occur. So much energy is wasted in hatred and disillusion, in envy, in malice, in wasted opportunity. Whole lives can come and go in aimless preoccupation with solely material needs, and those things of the spirit, those things which are eternal, are passed by and not heeded. But even these lives have their place in the scheme of things, for when the soul returns to the sphere it has inherited from its attack on life, it can see for itself the wasted effort spent in years which could have been put to so much better use.

Those who have had many spiritual lives and who have a heightened awareness of what should be done can see this waste in others. It is their inherent duty to try to show the material soul, not so much the error of its ways, but to open for it the doors of illumination and of light.

Free will

Q: Can I ask to what extent we have free will, because spirit seems to accurately know what will happen in our future?

Free will! We would like, if we may, to rephrase that saying. You have been given will – will to decide in what measure you will control your lives. The amount of freedom that you have is governed again by your karmic debts, by the body that you are inhabiting, and by the purpose behind this particular life.

There is a guidance, you are right. The guidance is the knowledge within the soul of what is past, the knowledge also of what is to be, and the fact that it is all part of 'the now'. The soul is aware of its ultimate lessons. It is aware as to how it is going to accomplish this end; it also knows that by following a certain pathway it can either impede or accelerate its progress.

The amount of freedom is contained within the soul. If it feels that a certain event or pastime is going to impede spiritual progress, it will not do this. If it feels that by remaining on a part of the globe it will be held back from that innate progress within it, it will move somewhere else. There will be an urgency within it which will accelerate the removal. If you have ever felt within yourself an urgency, a feeling that what you are doing is either very right or completely wrong, it is the knowledge of the soul within you which is pushing this forward. It is presenting itself as a thought or as a desire. You have free will, my son, within the structure of your karmic debt.

Light streams

In order to explain regarding the light streams, we will begin where all things begin, and that is with creation. We have spoken earlier of the nature of God so we will assume that this is acceptable to those who wish to have further teaching regarding the universe.

From God emanates all that is, and the light structure that is so easily analysed scientifically upon the Earth is part of that creative impulse of energy which first began, and from which all that is universal has grown. Each of the different light particles has its own meaning, its own task you might say and so it is quite important to be able to analyse this.

Take first the simple structure of the rainbow; every schoolchild is aware of what causes the rainbow and how beautiful its structure is. The same principle is called into play regarding each of the light streams that accord with the rainbow. Within the structure, each one has its own task, its own importance regarding the levels of energies. So from the beginning of time we have these different wavelengths of colour and they expand and grow from the central source.

Picture in your mind a dot of energy, of white light. From this in all directions as though you are looking at a flat surface, the rays of colour move outwards. They move into infinity. They are also joined together by the many different tones and shades of those colours. So there is awareness as you look at this one sheet of colour of its many cadences and many shades.

In circles around and through these streams of colour are ribbons of light. Because they are circular and are rotating around the central dot of light, they seem to separate these colours at intervals. At first they are very close and then as they expand and move into the distance, the distance between these bands of light increases, until you are looking upon a combined structure, an interweaving of colour and of light.

Each colour has its own task, as we have said before. There are different kinds of awareness within the soul. The soul itself emanates from that central light which is God, and at first it flowed within these streams of colour and light being merely inanimate, just part of this colour without any thought, any awareness or any living energy. But when it was intended that the soul should indeed have life, that it should have energy, make choices regarding its abilities and needs, and understand the life that is within spirit and compare it with that which is within the world, then the animation began.

At this time the ribbons of light interweaving in a circular manner began also to animate soul so that the light itself appeared to glow, to glisten, to move within itself so that the life within it became more and more radiant. The streams of colour responded likewise, the flatness of those colours ceased; there was living vibrancy. So now within your mind you can see this vibrant kaleidoscope of colour and light, impregnated by the reality of soul as it moves within the heart of God. From this all things stream.

The aura

The colour spectrum, which is the result of light, has its meaning for all. Each individual colour is reflected in yourself, for your soul is portrayed in the aura around you, and as you are, so is your aura. If you are gentle and kind, considerate to others, your aura reflects much pink. If you have psychic ability and are able to see far beyond the everyday occurrences, there will be much mauve within your aura. Those who have the healing ability, who can draw through themselves the energies from the higher spheres, their aura will reflect blues of varying intensity, according to the depth of their healing ability; and those who have found within themselves quiet alignment and unity, have green of perfect balance.

These colours are not like strokes upon a palette with paint. They flicker and intermingle, one with another, glowing, glittering, moving gently, as would the wind, around and around the body, fluctuating in and out, touching one another as you sit together in the body of this hall. Those with the healing ability are transmitting through their auras this wonderful sense of release to their neighbour. But those who have tensions, problems which they cannot come to terms with, those who bear malice to others, or even hatred, can show in their auras shades from the palest grey to the darkest black. Those who have the darkest colours within their auras are truly unhappy people in an intensely material incarnation, and unless they are helped to understand by more enlightened fellows and friends, when they return to the spirit world it will be to the lowest sphere, whence they will need to climb again to greater heights through their own efforts.

The aura and the body

We would also like to speak with you concerning the aura surrounding each part of your body. Each cell and organ within you vibrates to a different colour: the heart to green, the pancreas to gold, the stomach to orange – a different tone of orange to the intestines – the mind to magenta and the higher consciousness to violet. The other shades mingle and intermingle in the lesser organs of the body. If one of these organs is removed because of disease, the others have to stretch their aura to try to replace the depleted energy. Over a period of time, an etheric double forms, filling the void and replacing the depletion. It takes many months to recover from operations fully, because the etheric counterpart has to work slowly to replace each cell and create energy into the void. The more major the operation, the greater the length of time before the patient is fully recovered.

The chakras
You are aware, all of you, of the main chakras in the body, are you not? The crown chakra is really the most important, for this has direct access to the Higher Consciousness. It is within this centre, and emanating from it, that all awareness of the spiritual paths of life emanates and enters. If this chakra is not aware of the emotion of spirituality, that life becomes a purely material one, and the purpose behind the incarnation can become lost. Very often, this particular chakra is not moved into existence until the second or third stage in life. During the earlier years, from birth to puberty, the soul anxiously comes to terms with its physical self. From then until the early thirties, it is again concerned with things of matter. After that, the awareness of spirit can reach it, and this is usually when the crown chakra becomes sensitive.

We go from that to the 'third eye'. This can be activated at any time from the moment of birth. The third eye is behind the brow, over the eyes, and the psychic awareness of young children denotes the sensitivity of this important chakra. It is of great importance that young children are not made to feel strange, or out of alignment, when their perception of beings from another world are strong.

The throat chakra is essential to the well-being of most other areas of the body. If people are emotionally disturbed, this reflects in the area of the throat, causing restriction, difficulty in swallowing and breathing, palpitations, and many other problems within the respiratory system of the body. It is a very important chakra for the healer.

The heart chakra governs all the arterial and venal system in the body. The heart is a very important organ, not the most important, but, as everybody is aware, if the heart does not receive oxygen, it ceases to beat, and life is extinct. So again, this chakra should receive great attention from the healer.

The solar plexus introduces harmony within the whole of the body structure, and if for any reason this is disorientated through emotional problems, or through difficult karma, the healer may have great difficulty in balancing this with the other chakras. It is a highly sensitive part of the human being. Great delicacy should be shown in the handling of this chakra.

Little is said of the chakra at the base of the spine, usually referred to as the 'Kundalini', but all baser emotions emanate from this chakra. The life force itself, the desire for procreation starts within this chakra. The sudden awakening of it through the hands of an inept healer or psychic can cause great emotional confusion around the aura and the central being of the personality. Once awakened, it should be allowed to develop naturally at its own pace. It usually occurs naturally at puberty, but if it is awakened through harsh methods earlier in life, or for some reason it is retarded in its development and is awakened later, there can be severe emotional problems associated with that chakra. Gentleness and awareness must be created through the hands of the healer or therapist when handling this most sensitive and volatile of centres.

Note: There is a chakra, just below the navel, often referred to as the sacral chakra. The Master is inclined to omit it from his descriptions as he says that it is not of major spiritual significance.

The single cell

We wish now to speak of the seed of life, and how it unites each individual person in spirit and in the world. The universe began with one thought – a seed, a cell, a cell of life in which was embodied all life, the total understanding of what would be throughout the entire universe as time progressed; it was an embryo, a prototype for all living manifestation. When it was the time for the Earth to be born, again it began as a cell and all thought and all understanding was within that cell.

It is repeated within mankind – one seed, and from it a child shall grow. When you give thought to that, that the most wonderful manifestation of all life dwells within one seed, almost too small to be seen and yet also, surrounding that seed, is Universal Law, is love. A child develops in that love, and the Higher Self, which is another seed from which the soul has grown, is in close communication with the seed of that child from the instant of conception.

Q: I'm trying to picture that cell as it was at the beginning.

M: To the contrary, you can have any image within your mind as long as you apply the knowledge that you're visualizing the single cell. A sharp point of light, golden light, is sufficient, anything which focuses your attention. It is better not to have a specific object as this can be counterproductive. But light itself, golden light or any of the primary colours, with strength and vibrancy and which has the ability, of course, to grow and to merge and break down into its many facets, is excellent for visualization. You can imagine a golden sphere as an appropriate image, to represent the single cell.

The Master recommends this form of visualization of the single cell as a powerful healing tool, both in self-healing and the healing of others, as, he says, this represents an image of perfection.

Evolution of animals and man
Humankind did not evolve exclusively from animal life. It was very near animal life – fur that covered the body was necessary for climatic conditions – and man has changed as the Earth has changed and as the climate has changed through its process of balance. At that time man would see very little differently from the animal world. The animal world sees shape, it does not see colour. It is not aware of humankind in the way that humans are aware of each other, but it can use its sense of smell. One human being may not be aware, consciously, of the smell of another. But the animal is very aware and can tell at some distance that which is familiar and that which is not. A domestic animal will know that a master or mistress is approaching when that person is perhaps three or four hundred yards away and cannot be seen. So in a way the animal world is more evolved regarding scents than human beings are within the world. We try to encourage mankind to be totally aware of his senses and not just those he relies on to exist. The animals that evolve so

much more slowly are so much better able to do this.

Q: So that in a sense humankind evolved as the Earth changed and evolved and not from an animal source?

M: That is so. That evolution was all part of the structural plan at the beginning of creation and it will continue until the end. That God force does know when the Earth will cease to exist in its present form. We do not know this but the God essence does know and there will be a time when the world will change and there will not be the form of life that is upon it as now.

You can compare humankind with animals if you wish. Animals work with instinct, they appear to have intelligence because the instinct provides all that is needed for survival. It provides cunning, for example, without which very few of the animal species (and this includes the fish world) would be able to survive the manoeuvres of other predatory species, but it is not capable of logic. Soul is capable of logic, but in the end it had to have a stabilizing force. It had to be provided with what has become humanity.

Time

At the beginning of time the soul was born of perfection. The all-knowing Universal Mind, in conceiving the perfection of the soul, could have allowed it to remain a thought in space, but the projection of this thought was such that progress in all things, for all eternity of time, inevitably began.

To understand the meaning of our concept of time, one needs a mind beyond the earthly comprehension. Even on the causal plane this is only reality as we are aware of it; there may be other realities beyond this. We can assume the knowledge and contemplation of the component of time, using the earthly mechanisms for this, is but a method derived by man to enable him to apportion his day, and relate to Universal Law – though he ultimately uses it to live according to his own interpretation of law.

Time is something that man considers important, but it cannot really be measured in such a way, for all time has already occurred; everything which moves within it is happening now, within this moment. If you can picture one of your cameras with the pictures you take, first one exposure, then another, until every picture upon the roll has been imprinted upon the film. When it is finished, it is removed from the camera and the negative developed, showing what occurred in one instant of time, imprinted forever upon that sheet of paper. This you were aware of as you took the picture, and you relive it again when it has been developed. Now it exists for you in the present. This is the simplest analogy that we feel able to give you when we try to explain that all cause and effect occurred at that one instant of thought, giving life to the universe. It is that as you travel through your lives, you are aware at that moment of the action, because that which motivates you can only perceive the 'now'.

The illusion of time

Several hundred years ago time was relatively different from the present. It is indeed becoming quicker, faster. One hour of time now is equivalent to three or four hours in the seventeenth century. Two thousand years ago a day was truly long. From sunrise to sunset so much could be achieved. Going back in the mind to those times, especially through regression, and moving into the soul's pattern in that manner, you can then experience the movement of time as it has accelerated throughout existence. It is now reaching its peak; the time for true knowledge and ability is here. There will never be a greater opportunity to contact the Higher Self through meditation, deliberation and prayer than man has been granted at this stage in his development. With the Aquarian Age, the time ratio will be completely different, as also will life upon the Earth as time passes.

The spiral of time

There has been much spoken and written regarding that which is taking place at this time and toward the age which is now commencing. There has also been much spoken regarding changes in vibrations – that of the Earth, the planetary systems, and most importantly within man himself. None of these things is new, but what is so often unacknowledged is the reason why it is taking place. Many ask a very simple question and yet in its simplicity there is great profundity also: 'Why now? Why at this time as an age approaches – the age of Aquarius – is there so much activity in the planetary and spiritual worlds and in preparation amongst mankind himself? Has this indeed occurred before when other ages approached?'

This particular age – the Aquarian Age – is one which will be of great fulfilment. It also marks the completion of a spiral of time. This may not be new to some of you; others may ask: 'What is a spiral of time?'. If you can imagine that at the commencement of the universe there was also the commencement of a spiral, a spiral of bright, beautiful light, a light which was manifest within the Cosmic Force, God or whatever word you use to describe the Creator of all, that is a pure, white energizing light of pure love.

This spiral of light gradually increased in its volume and in its brightness. As with all spirals, as they increase with speed they become more and more akin to a circle, a circle that is blazing with colour, all the colours of the spectrum and the many shades which are depicted within those colours. Imagine them if you will, turning at speed, the wonderful brightness being depicted as a cascade of stars into that supreme darkness, that void. Gradually, as the planetary life was created and took its place within the universe, these brilliant lights extended toward them. Anyone who was viewing this spectacular display would, in this day and age, be reminded of fireworks, each wonderful colour emitting its own spark of brilliance.

Toward the end of the first age (remember that each age has a duration of two thousand years) this spiral of activity reached its peak. All the vibrations within the universe had reached a total speed for that particular age. Then there comes the time when another age approaches. When this takes place, the universe again slows down very greatly. The colours separate; they are akin to the colours depicted within the chakras, which commence at the first chakra with a very dark red, moving upwards until eventually there is this pure golden colour merging into the whiteness of the bright, diamond-toned light. Each facet of light is distinct on its own and those that were then present upon the Earth would need to be aware of those colours within themselves, the growth of the personality, the growth of that age and in what way it would be necessary for man to learn.

A learning process
All of life for mankind is a learning process. When the body is released and it goes again within the soul and ascends to the spiritual spheres, the lesson of that life is then complete. The soul is then on a much higher and faster vibration, the colours within the aura depict within their vibrancy the progress that each individual soul has made, and this vibrancy is collected

within this spiral of light and thus intensifies its beauty. So mankind with all his personality, his soul body, and that of the universe itself, are all one within the light.

As that particular age draws to its climax and then is closed, the whole process commences again. In the millions of years since the creation began, this process has continued. The one eternal spiral, that which is of the God force, has also reached a great peak of intensity. The age to come, that of Aquarius, marks the completion of a whole universal era of progress. At the completion of the next two thousand or so years, man's ability for intelligence will peak; his ability to be the custodian of his world will reach a peak also. Whether the world continues or begins to fail depends upon man's acceptance of that role and his ability to overcome his own weakness and allow the world to once again retain its strength and its beauty as the creation had depicted.

Because of this weakness within man, this desire always for the free will to be the strength of man, thus being his weakness, those who dwell in the spirit spheres within the causal plane (which is the plane of the mind, of the intelligence) those Masters and Teachers of Light have decided among themselves that man now needs help.

Atlantis

Millions of years ago there was a great continent within the world. At least two thirds of the world was known as Atlantis. Remove from your minds for one moment all stories that you have heard of one small island and what occurred to it. What we are now to say is the truth. Many of our group were present at intervals during the life of this great continent, and many of you also, at different periods over the millions of years. Facets of your souls were born and died and new facets were born again. We do not speak of a brief period of time; we speak of millions of years. We speak of an era of history little known to man, although more and more evidence is coming to light as ancient documents are being resurrected from long-forgotten tombs, and as more are able to link their minds clairvoyantly with others on the inner planes who can teach and give their wisdom and understanding accordingly.

Eight hundred thousand years before the time that you are now enjoying, this continent had spread in great proportions. The whole of Europe, where you now live, was part of it. It spread and took in the wonderful land of Egypt where so much learning and wisdom took place. The people who lived within these lands had great powers. They walked upon the land and yet their minds linked with the spirit spheres.

Gradually as we come nearer to the present time, the peoples changed. They became more aware of their freedom of expression, that they could change their surroundings at their own will, that they did not always need spiritual guidance. There were those that came into the world full of power, and they looked towards the darkness for their knowledge. Many who ruled, ruled with wisdom, but there were those that, using the occult or the dark arts, as they are known, were able through sheer power to manipulate the minds of mankind.

Where there is evil and the worshipping of evil, there is destruction. The law of the universe is implicit in this ... When the great floods came, all the land, temples and monuments that were within that land were covered by the ocean. Ten thousand years ago, the first of the floods took place. There was a flood eighty thousand years before that, which destroyed much of what had become known as Atlantis. Those that fled from the torrents took up their abode in high lands. There they continued to give of their influence and their learning and tried to give to tribes that knew nothing some form of knowledge and learning which they had brought from their beautiful cities.

However, ten thousand years ago, the evil reached a peak. No longer could the Masters on the inner plane that worked with the creative impulse allow the world to continue upon its course. There was a series of what we term natural disasters – the repeat of these have been taking place within your world at this time. One small part of this huge continent remained, and even this eventually was submerged.

Some Atlanteans escaped in boats and made their way to Egypt where they founded the great dynasties of the Pharaohs. Those that did not, passed to spirit where the lessons they had learned were assimilated within their Higher Selves. It is this understanding and knowledge that is now being shared again through the Children of Light.

It is in your deep subconscious mind that you will remember ... Use your knowledge, my children, that those things that were good within that time may be recreated within your lifetime and beyond.

The Children of Light

There is now a generation where some of the souls that are incarnating have not done so for millions of years, since the time of Atlantis. They last dwelled upon the Earth when the souls were still able to commune with the higher spiritual realms and when the mind of man was not so limited and tethered by his ignorance.

These souls have been born in the same way as any other child has been born, but there is a difference. Mankind from the moment of birth has no memory of the past, no memory of a spiritual existence and no memory of a past existence on the Earth, therefore that young new child begins life ignorant of life, and needs to progress in the same way as it has done for millions of years. But these children (we call them the Children of Light or the Aquarian Children, if this pleases you) they have memory, memory of the spiritual lives that they have enjoyed upon the Earth, and memory also of the spiritual life in the spheres of light.

These children will grow as others do. When they reach maturity they will be the leaders, the teachers; they will be those that will represent the leaders of the countries. Gradually they, and those that are born from them, will prevent the wars, the destruction that has begun to envelop the world. All that is occurring now is within the great plan of life. The many millions of souls which now inhabit the Earth are due to return to spirit, to enhance themselves once more in their etheric soul bodies, and they will not return again to the Earth until it is stabilized, until once more it is a place of beauty and learning. It will be inhabited instead mostly by these Children of Light, many of whom are still being born, many of whom are presently approaching adulthood.

There will, of course, also be many others that are born, but the souls within them will be aware of their task to rehabilitate the Earth. The many different countries within the continents upon the Earth will be more sparsely populated, and this is having an impact already – the internal wars within the countries, with so many returning to spirit. Other continents will find similar events occurring, the 'natural disasters', so-called, the earthquakes, the flooding, the erosion of land by the oceans, this is all part of the cycle of life for the completion of this present age – the Piscean Age.

The extract above came from a talk the Master gave during the 1980s. Now, in the year 2001, the transition to the Aquarian Age is complete.

The Children of Light now beginning to grow still have many years before adulthood, before their integral wisdom permits them to change the law of man and instate in its place the spiritual law of true understanding and purpose; but when eventually they take their place within the governments of the world, then the anticipated changes will begin to take place. Many hundreds of years must pass before even their efforts will show within the world itself, so great has been the neglect, the devastation of this beautiful planet.

The Children of Light, as they grow, will not need reminding as much as man of the past. Their spiritual understanding is such that they will walk their paths rigidly, aware totally of the light that guides them, and this will spread to those whom they seek to help and guide. It will be an interesting time, and those of you who will be combining your efforts with these children will be an essential part of life in the next decades and able to compare then with now. Still you must have awareness of those who are limited in what their soul desires to achieve. There are still many living who have come upon the spiral at a time when the world is less advanced, and they cannot change their opinions and their destiny as much as those with greater spiritual understanding.

The Children of Light will have far less difficulty in understanding mankind than man will have in accepting these children, who have such special qualities and who will have such tasks to perform. It is difficult to believe that such very young people, as they are now, will develop such ability.

Rays and archangels
Each age has a predominant colour, and those that are born within an age are those that are linked with particular colour rays. Throughout the Piscean Age it has been those of the purple ray. The divine force which has linked man with God has been Uriel, Archangel of Light, manifesting within the purple ray. In the age now just begun, the Aquarian Age, it will be the golden ray. The Children of Light are of this ray and their Master of Light is Michael, Archangel of the Golden Ray; and so this continues in the different ages. The wisdom is from the

one God force; its representation is through the divine knowledge which has been bestowed upon the Archangels, and the way that they themselves can allow man to go forward in evolution, learning, portraying, sharing, distributing. All have a particular rhythm, all move within a particular spiral of activity.

The legacy of the Piscean Age

The Piscean Age is worth a mention. It is the most advanced age since man inhabited the Earth. It is a scientific age. All that is occurring now has been inspired by the knowledge within the spirit spheres. Mankind tunes in with his brain and thus inventions occur, and upon the Earth the beautiful things which are present in certain spirit spheres are then replicated.

Unfortunately, man has freedom of choice; he can use these beautiful inventions for peace, or he can use them to annihilate, to destroy. Man is the only species who has free will. The animal world has instinct, and very primitive early man had instinct also. It was when man was given this precious gift in order to use his intelligence, to build a world toward the spirit spheres, that many of the problems which now exist began.

Many upon the world at this time greatly fear the future. There are many who have predicted the end of the world will come quite soon – massive earthquakes, destruction by wars, flooding by the oceans, by torrential rain. Do not heed them. Although spirit finds it extremely difficult to measure time, as they live in a timeless state of being, there are guidelines which apply. There is a time within the ages when certain effects must take place, when others must be completed, when man must reach a certain stage in his development and then begin to transform and change, to become more aware, more spiritual in his being. This is known to the Masters of Light, therefore it is known that even man with his free will cannot destroy the Earth until a certain time has passed.

Because of these Children of Light, their intervention, the great power which will be bestowed upon them, it is very, very unlikely that the world will perish. It will revert to its first beauty, and man will again be master of all he surveys, but with an inner understanding of his task and his commitment.

Q: I would like to ask the Master if he has some advice for us about the future, the time that is coming?

M: To be at peace within yourselves, to be assured that God's plan and purpose will progress. There is none that is greater than God, therefore there are none that have a greater power, either within the world or within a sphere of light, or a planet. By understanding this, by using an affirmation for the creation of peace and light, in that way all will go forward into the future without even more calamity than man has manifested for himself by his actions.

Do remember, the actions of today bring forth the results of the morrow. The more people there are with belief, with a concentrated awareness of action for the future, the greater the overcoming of evil from those with no belief, or those that are intent upon destruction – and there are many millions more who believe in peace and life everlasting, than those who desire destruction.

Appendix II

Earth-healing visualizations
The Master suggested I include the following visualizations to precede the Earth-healing meditation, which is done at 10 pm British time at the time of the full and the new moon. The more people that join in this meditation at the same time, the more powerful its effect.

G: As we are discussing our connection with the Earth, we do mention the Earth-healing meditation earlier in the book. Would it be a good thing to include in the book so that the people who are inspired to do this could actually share in that process on the full and the new moon?

M: Indeed yes.

G: So would you have a special visualization for them to do?

M: It is better to give them a simple process of visualization, the way that we already do this with those that come and speak with us in this manner and who ask for visualizations for healing the self and to assist the planet. There are now many hundreds that join in at this time so it is very good to put this within the book as a means of linking, so that all those who wish to harmonize with nature can do so. The visualization that most people seem to find the most powerful is to do with nature.

There is the autumn linking, which is the walking through a gate into the woodland. The peace, the stillness, is disturbed only by the crunching of leaves beneath the feet. They pause to tune into nature, to hear the leaves flutter to the ground where they rest. The small little creatures in the undergrowth scurry from one place to another, seeking their sustenance to store for the cold winter months. The sun filters through the fast-emptying branches as they look upwards, feeling the cooler crisper air on their faces as they walk.

Or there is also the spring walk, entering by the same gate, looking up at all the branches of the trees just bursting into bud. They hear the sound of the birds as they sing joyously, build their nests and raise their young. The stronger rays of sun warm the face and the firm ground beneath the feet, hardened by the winter frosts, has not yet been softened by the warm summer rain.

These two are particularly powerful because they show the difference between a time approaching for peace, regeneration, rest, and the awakening, the springing into life, the purpose to go forward. These are the two seasons we concentrate upon the most greatly for man to be aware of, to look forward to. Of course to that visualization you can then add the meditation process which you are already familiar with.

The Earth-healing meditation
Sound 12 times the mantra 'Aum Shekinah', after which you imagine a beam of pearlescent golden light descending in a spiral upon you, surrounding you and moving down into the Earth. Visualize the golden light spiralling down below you into the Earth, moving down into the soil, the sub-soil and the bedrock beneath.

See the light gaining momentum as it travels ever faster into the molten core of the planet and on towards the very centre of the Earth. At the centre of the Earth imagine a crystal, the Mother Crystal of the Earth, which bursts into life as the golden spiral reaches it.

This Crystal, now glowing like the Sun, radiates light in all directions, back up through the molten core and all the strata of the Earth. See this light enlivening the crystalline structures that are there and moving into the areas of the Earth where there is potential for volcanic eruptions and earthquakes. Imagine these being bathed in gold and green light so that they cool down and dissipate harmlessly.

The light now moves onward into the soil, nourishing and healing all living things: the ecosystem, plant life, the animal and insect kingdoms. See it illuminating the waters of the planet, bringing healing and cleansing.

Allow the light to move into the hearts and minds of man, so that areas of conflict and disaster may be helped and uplifted, and peace may prevail on Earth.

The light moves out into the atmosphere, cleansing the air we breathe and repairing the damage to the ozone layer.

See the whole planet bathed in golden light as it radiates out across the solar system, across the galaxy to the edges of the universe and back to source.

THE WAY OF TRUTH

Index

A

Absolute, 83, 143; Great, 145; truth, 68, 70; zero, 105
Adam and Eve, 110, 119
Affirmation, 165
Age(s), 11, 27, 44, 60, 61, 159, 160; Aquarian, 88, 135, 146, 158, 163; Golden, 11, 57, 113; New; 138
AIDS, 57
Akashic records, 147
Alignments, planetary, 114
Amethyst, 19, 80
Angel, 17, 100; fallen, 106
Animals, 79, 80, 81, 94; & instinct; & man, 156; regeneration, 100, 101; reincarnation 119
Antimatter, 40, 44, 46, 49, 51, 53, 91
Archangel, Michael, 113, 163; of the golden ray, 163; of light, 163
Aspect, of love, 65; of soul, 16, 24, 61, 81, 124, 149
Astral, 86, 87; plane, 86, 87, 148, 153; travelling, 54
Astrological age, 83; Aquarian, 88, 135,158, 163; first, 159; legacy of, 164; Piscean, 135, 164
Atlanteans, 110; civilization, 112; times, 121
Atlantis, 84, 109, 110, 160, 161, 162; & Lemuria, 110
Atomic, bomb, 112, 114; engine house, 131; force, 102; particles, 33; structures, 23, 32, 33, 34
Atom(s), 23, 25, 46, 47, 56, 74, 102; split, 28
Aquarian Age, 88, 135, 146, 158, 160; children, 162
Arimathea, Joseph of, 17
Aum, 30, 103, 127, 143, 144, 167; & the music of the spheres, 103; & Shekinah, 124, 167
Aura(s), 52, 78, 98, 153, 155, 159; of the body, 98; of mankind, 142; of the planets, 93
Autumn, equinox, 135; linking, 166

B

Bearer of light, 100, 107
Beings, first, 54; of light, 65, 110, 144; planetary, 13, 93, 104
Big Bang, 60, 108, 109; and spirit spheres, 108
Birth, 16, 17, 23, 27, 110, 119, 128, 130, 154; of Jesus, 149
Black, 153; holes, 47, 48, 49, 51, 52, 64, 103
Blueprint, 32, 34, 73, 75, 101
Bodies, corporate, 117; & soul, 65; subtle, 99
Bomb, atomic, 112, 114
Brain, 27, 28, 29, 30, 33, 34, 38, 39, 49, 50, 56, 61, 70, 77, 82, 98, 104, 109, 136, 144, 164; and mind, 27, 77

C

Cancer, 129

Index

Devil, 107
Deys, 127
Diamond light, 159
Dimension(s), 52, 53, 60; etheric, 93; fourth, 55; spatial, 60
Dinosaur(s), 24, 27, 63, 72, 83, 94, 109; & parallel universes, 54
Disease(s), 100, 154; life threatening, 129
Divine link, 109
DNA, 41, 101, 130
Dogma, 136, 137, 138; business, 138; political, 138
Dreams, 55, 58, 61; lucid, 53
Dreamless sleep, 146

E

Earth, Aquarian Age, 158; basic principle, 92; calamities, 90; and causal plane, 77; and Children of Light, 162; and man, 25, 28, 29,. 86, 87, 88, 118, 121, 122, 156, 157; atmosphere, 98; chaotic principle, 91; centre, 59; collective mind, energy changes, 135; evolution, 94, 109, 111; feminine, 130; healing meditation, 59, 123, 124, 166, 167; Lucifer; 106, more than one, 46, 51; and planetary system, 41, 45, 91, 96, 97, 99, 100, 102, 105; place of learning, 86, 94, 144, 145, 148, 149; planet, earth, 86, 91; plates of, 111; regeneration, 122; sound, 127; spheres of light, 37, 52, 63, 93, 116, 149; sphere of matter, 36; spiral, 60
Earthquakes, 118, 162, 164, 167
Egypt(ian), 84, 106, 110, 161
Eldars, 54, 55, 110, 127
Electrical impulses, 37, 98
Electron, 25, 33, 46, 49, 74
Elements, 25, 34, 88, 97, 100, 144
Elohim, 54
Els, 54, 110
Embryo, 132, 140
Emotional body, 81
End of world, 59, 164
Energy, 21, 48, 59, 60, 75, 83, 94, 95, 96, 100, 146, 150, 153, 154; complete, 145; exchange, 99; field, 22, 25, 31, 109; hierarchical structure of, 128; intelligent, 94; kinetic, 22; living, 61, 95; negative, 92, 115; of God, 81; of the Moon, 81; positive & negative, 92, 115; pulsing, 149; spiritual, 89, 98; vibrational, 25
Entropy, 62
Environment, 134, 140; influencing, 58
Equinox, autumn, 135; spring, 135
Erosion of land, 162
Etheric, the, 52, 77, 83, 87, 154; being, 147; body, 73; dimension, 94; personality, 54; self, 17, 55, 148; sense, 62; soul, 162; world, 78
Ethics, 58, 123

THE WAY OF TRUTH

THE WAY OF LOVE

*Joseph of Arimathea tells the True Story
behind the Message of Jesus*

Compiled by Peter Wheeler

The truth about Jesus the man and Jesus the Christ is told by Joseph of Arimathea through a deep-trance medium. He is acting as a spokesman for a group of souls including certain Apostles and other major figures concerning those remarkable events of 2,000 years ago. This makes this book unique.

Joseph – the Arimathean – an uncle of Jesus, master-minded His education as a young man. The complete story of Jesus the Christ is revealed – much of it through the past lives of people living today – together with Essenic teachings which so strongly influenced Christ's own message, the Teachings of the Way. Some of the past lives have been specially selected because they paint a vivid word picture of how life was under Roman occupation. This book is for all who seek the Truth and the Light, be they Christian, Jewish, Moslem or those with no religious faith.

**256 pages paperback.
ISBN 90-75635-01-X.**

THE MEMORIES OF JOSEPHES

Soul Memories of a Cousin of Jesus

David Davidson

This book is made up of the memories of Josephes, the eldest son of Joseph of Arimathea. During meditation David Davidson began to see vivid glimpses of the life and times of Josephes, who lived 2,000 years ago in Jerusalem and Cyprus. What makes these memories special is that Josephes was a cousin of Yeshua (Jesus) who was his constant boyhood companion and lifelong confidant.

Over the course of three and a half years the story of Josephes' life emerged, chronicling his struggles, his intense relationship with his cousin and his own ultimate death.

This book presents a beautiful, poetic and dramatic account, not just of the life of Josephes but also of the trials of Yeshua as he grew, realised, and fulfilled his destiny. It is a book that can be read either as a complete story or as a series of discrete images which are ideal for meditation.

256 pages paperback.
ISBN 0-9532007-0-1.

THE WAY OF CRYSTALS

Joseph of Arimathea and the Prophet Elijah

Compiled by Zanne Findlay

As humanity enters the Golden Age, crystals and crystal healing are achieving a renaissance. In past civilisations they have been the basis of medicine, regeneration, science and power; they are literally portals to the spirit realm. They can be used for healing, as an aid to meditation, for protection, stimulating past-life memories and creating ambience.

This unique book combines the channelled words of two spiritual Masters, Joseph of Arimathea and the Prophet Elijah. Both have a profound insight into crystals and healing and have never before been published on this subject. Their words, woven together with the practical experience of Zanne Findlay, make this book authoritative at the same time as being simple, clear and pragmatic.

Each one of the techniques presented here has been proven by the author who has tried and tested them; both on her courses and with individual clients. This book will appeal to healers and to anyone who has an interest in the beauty and healing power of crystals.

Healing handbook, 160 pages paperback, with illustrations. ISBN 0-9532007-5-2.

THE CHILDREN OF LIGHT

Father Abraham on the Fulfilment of a Prophecy

Compiled by David Davidson

The Children of Light are already among us. They are highly intuitive, with eyes that betray an understanding and wisdom far beyond their years. Their deep inner knowing and innate sense of purpose means that they don't take kindly to direction or discipline. On the other hand they grow and glow in the presence of love.

These children, the eldest already adults, are different from the rest of humanity in two important respects; firstly, they are souls who have finished their round of incarnation and so have no Karma. Secondly, they have access to the knowledge of their entire Higher Selves. They are spiritual elders, incarnating now in response to the environmental, political and economic crises that face humanity.

In this compilation of channelling Father Abraham of the Old Testament talks of their needs, their purpose and how to recognise and help them in their tasks. This book will appeal to all who have an involvement with children and young people, to parents, teachers and all those with an interest in the spiritual wellbeing of humanity.

Monograph, 96 pages paperback.
ISBN 0-9532007-2-8.

THE WAY OF SOUL

Compiled by David Davidson

In this channelled book, Joseph of Arimathea, uncle and guardian of the young Yeshua, who was to become Jesus the Christ, acts as spokesperson for figures such as Father Abraham, the Prophet Elijah. As he speaks he maps out a spiritual architecture that towers above creation like a cathedral of light.

The nature of God, the origin of soul, the spheres of light and life after death, parallel worlds, reincarnation and the purpose of life itself, all are discussed from the perspective of soul. Step by step he takes us through the stages of creation to this critical turning point in history and how best we can manage the challenges it presents us.

With additions from over twenty years of his teaching this book creates a clear picture of the place and progress of humanity as part of a vast spiritual reality. It will be of interest to all with an inquiring mind, whether philosophical, scientific, religious or artistic by nature, for the truths contained within these pages transcend the boundaries of culture or religion.

Monograph, 128 pages paperback.
ISBN 0-9532007-4-4.

DISCOURSES WITH MALACHI

Opening to spiritual guidance

David Davidson

During morning meditations David Davidson began a mental dialogue with a spiritual teacher named Malachi. Over the course of the next three years Malachi explained exactly how and why this dialogue was happening.

This book is primarily about the relationship between two people: one, a spiritual teacher who lived eight thousand years ago and one, a psychologist who is alive now. Malachi speaks with authority, depth and compassion but as he does so he tests David's beliefs to the point of making him wish he had never started.

This book provides a valuable guide and handbook for those who wish to enter into a dialogue with spirit. The addition of Malachi's predictions, his patience and his rather dry sense of humour make his explanations about how spirit communicates with humankind both inspiring and thought-provoking. Many who have read it find it provides an ideal 'thought for the day'.

Monograph, 128 pages paperback.
ISBN 0-9532007-6-0.

The Arimathean Foundation

The Leaders Partnership is the imprint of the Arimathean Foundation. The Foundation has been established to publish and disseminate the channelled teachings of a group of Spiritual Teachers. This group includes Joseph of Arimathea, Elijah, Father Abraham and also the Prophet Malachi. All the Teachers in this group work within the light of the Christos, the love aspect of God. They were instrumental in enabling this to incarnate as a man, watched over him as he walked the Earth and acknowledge him as their Lord and Teacher. All are now Masters in the spheres of light.

In addition to this Josephes, companion and confidant to the young Christ, has added his insight to the body of knowledge and wisdom that these books represent.

To order these books

These books are available from selected bookshops and
can be ordered through any bookshop with Whitakers or
Bookdata ordering systems.

To order direct from the publisher send a stamped
addressed envelope for an order form to:

The Leaders Partnership
Box 16457
London SE14 5WH

LP

NOTES

NOTES

NOTES

NOTES

NOTES